Selling
CHANGE

Robert E. Smith, Ph.D.

To order additional copies of this book, contact:
Xlibris
1-888-795-4274
www.Xlibris.com
Orders@Xlibris.com
780793

Selling
CHANGE

How Successful Leaders Use Impact, Influence, and Consistency to Transform Their Organizations

Robert E. Smith, Ph.D.

Contents

Praise for *Selling Change*

Selling Change is not the typical change management book dedicated to packaging past ideas with new flair. Instead, it admits the shortcoming of prior models in today's volatile and ever changing business environment. *Selling Change* finds the best of the past and builds on it while providing practical new approaches backed by research and cross-industry best practices. With the tools this provides you really can put a price on the value of change management. This is a must read for change practitioners and leaders of change programs alike.
--Scott Smith, Senior Director - Talent Management and Organization Development, PepsiCo

"Robert's book is timely and relevant. He takes us on a journey through real-life change in organizations. And he is able to blend theory and research to provide a practical application. The 2IsC™ change path is simple to apply. In the midst of an acquisition, I was able to take tools from this book and apply them real-time. Robert is able to address individual change within the context of organizational change. Previous models of change focus on individual change or organization change, leaving professionals to bridge the gap. The 2IsC™ Model addresses the gap and makes it possible to improve change outcomes."
--Gretchen Thompson, Principle Human Resource Project Manager, C.H. Robinson

"When leading change one needs to bring their team along on the journey. Gone are the days of the change hero, doing it all alone. *Selling Change* provides an actionable, implementable way to create the buy-in needed for sustained change success. I use these methods and they work!"
- Joe Raasch, Director, Minnesota Office of Continuous Improvement

"As a leader responsible for supporting people processes in a complex organizational setting, one of the biggest lessons from the book is the importance of managing stakeholder expectations and emotions during the early phases of change planning (even before impacted stakeholders decide to commit to the change and demonstrate new ways of working) and throughout each stage of the change process. Robert explores change management through real-world case studies, not just theory. This is important because leaders are starving for examples and tips to effectively lead their change initiatives; not more static templates and tools. The book does a superb job of bringing together all three while avoiding over-complicated analysis which made it simple to read cover to cover in an afternoon. I recommend *Selling Change* to any leader looking for a fresh perspective on leading change and practical tips in how to make change a reality in their workplace."

--LaTranda Martin, Organization Design and Change Management Director, The Estee Lauder Companies, Inc.

This book provides a practical and useful new change management playbook that addresses how to avoid failures as found in 60% - 70% of organization change initiatives. It is a "must read" for change agents.

----Andrew H. Van de Ven, Professor Emeritus, Carlson School of Management, University of Minnesota

"Being 'born' from asking the question: 'How do we get people to commit to organizational changes that could result in the worst possible outcome for them personally—the loss of a job?' the 2IsC™ Model is thought provoking and challenges conventional change management thinking. In *Selling Change*, Smith challenges change leaders to communicate the need for organizational change using impact, influence, and consistency. The focus on outcomes-focused organizational change is critical given the rapid pace of change we face every day.

--Ettienne B. Bouwer, Director Human Resources, Gallo Glass Company

Dedication

To those who came before, my parents, Helen and Jerome—
the most hard-working, *impactful* people I know.

To those who come after, my boys—the
most *consistent* early risers I know.

Introduction

We live in an age of near-perpetual organizational change. If your organization has not yet started a new change or transformation effort, it is probably smack in the middle of an existing one or planning for the next big one. Be it a shift to Agile processes, a culture change, opening in a new market, or adapting to digital transformation, organizations of all sizes and types are in the midst of massive transformation. So why another book on leadership and organizational change, you ask? Let's first consider the very relevant statistic that over half (52%) of Fortune 500 organizations have merged, declared bankruptcy, been acquired, are on the verge of irrelevancy or have simply gone under since 2000.[1] Notable cases include Eastman Kodak, Circuit City, Rhythm in Motion (Blackberry), Barnes and Noble, Radio Shack, Blockbuster, Toshiba, and most recently, Toys R Us. These were all once powerhouse brands whose products and services many reading these words frequented and are (or were) well-established household names. On one hand, it could be said that these organizations had their time yet with the winds of change, technology enhancements, changing customer expectations and strong competition, these institutions lost relevancy to their consumer base. On the other hand, each of these organizations' stories are sorted and fraught with possibilities and missed opportunities to make different sets of strategic and tactically-focused decisions to turn things around and truly commit themselves to transforming the way they ran. On the government side, the story does not appear to be much better. U.S. states including Illinois, Connecticut, Kentucky, New Jersey, and Massachusetts have been identified as potentially unable to meet their pension and other key financial obligations though few would argue that any of these areas are strangers to business development or historically have had difficulty attracting commerce or property taxes.[2] Organizations of all types will continue to experience constant and accelerated change and those that fail to adapt and transform will become irrelevant or face extinction. Unfortunately, many organizations are painfully bad at transforming themselves. The pesky statistic that 70% of organizational changes fail persists, suggesting that even when organizational leaders do identify the need for change and attempt to make those changes a reality in their organizations, the vast majority are unsuccessful.[3] A deeper look into the causes of change failure does not reveal a lack of resources or poor planning being the primary culprits, but instead, a lack of buy-in to those changes from the people needed to execute organizational change. Simply put, the people involved in attempts to change the organization's direction were not engaged in or they actively resisted the proposed changes. I believe this is due to the fact that more often than not, organizational change is not sold well. In other words, when leaders propose organizational transformations, they fail to do so in ways that get people to buy-in to the need for the change or transformation efforts. This results in organizations instituting "zombie" changes in which team members go through the motions of change but do not actually change their behaviors or attitudes in meaningful ways. These change initiatives then limp along, never fully realizing their potential.

Selling Change challenges some of the long-standing paradigms of organizational change by introducing commitment into the change management process. Rather

"[without commitment] … organizations institute 'zombie' changes in which organizational members go through the motions of change but do not actually change their behaviors or attitudes in meaningful ways"

than simply following a set of standardized change and communication process steps that focus more on change leader's actions and their desired goals we instead explore a new, research-based model and stories of successful organizational transformations across a variety of industries from manufacturing, to retail, to healthcare that follow the principles of highly engaged change commitment. This approach is more focused on those who must execute change in their organizations and what they need to successfully buy into and execute change. The research highlighted in this book describes how change leaders at these organizations achieve the most highly engaged levels of commitment to change and do so in ways that provide the information needed for team members to 'want to' commit to change.

The rate of change is increasing at an exponential pace with the convergence of changing client demands, new technologies, new ways of working, and changing employee expectations. The organizations that will survive and thrive into the future are those that are led by transformational leaders who can galvanize their teams by articulating the need for and impact of organizational changes needed make their organizations future-ready. In a world where the challenge of widespread, transformational organizational change has become so daunting that prominent organizational researchers have begun proposing the idea of simply creating separate organizations within organizations with their own leadership teams, funding streams, and decision-making models, gaining an understanding of how to get multiple stakeholder groups to commit to transformational change is no small undertaking.[4],[5] While approaches to transformational organizational change that rely on creating separate organizations within organizations can work and has been tried before, it is a bit of a cynical and defeatist approach. These models harken back to the days of widespread corruption in US cities and police departments that led to the rise of institutions such as the Federal Bureau of Investigation (FBI). Before the establishment of the FBI, local police departments were so corrupt that even leaders who were genuinely committed to making changes in their departments would hit a wall of resistance in the middle layer, stymying them from making any real changes. Internal anti-mob, off-the-record police units were set up like the famous "Untouchables" to get around the problem of corrupt (and corruptible) officers and lieutenants. These groups became the heroes who served the true missions of these organizations. Is this really the state of large modern-day organizations? To affect change, separate and distinct internal groups need to be set up to serve real and changing consumer needs and demands? Perhaps, but what if there was a different way? What if there was a way to modify existing organizational structures and gain enough buy-in across multiple stakeholder groups -from finance, to product design, to IT- to affect widespread organizational change and achieve change results that are well-above the 30% success rate we see today? High performing change leaders are demonstrating the ability to effectively transform their organizations. My research, along with leading research in the field of organizational change, shows that frequently, the only difference between successful change organizations and more intransigent, change-resistant organizations is the fact that organizations that achieve successful transformations have leaders who have tapped into a set of practices, behaviors, and leadership styles that lend themselves to more effective transformation outcomes. Perhaps we need to revisit the way change agents talk about, approach, and build consensus for change in their organizations. I am convinced that highly engaged change commitment is the key to achieving those outcomes. People who demonstrate highly engaged change commitment demonstrate a willingness to learn new ways of doing things, have higher levels of performance, and are involved in change projects that show higher rates of successful outcomes.

The Power of Organizational Change

If you could create one human invention that was capable of putting a person on the moon, eradicating diseases that less than 100 years ago killed thousands of children annually, mapping the human genome, and creating an audio-visual library containing most of all recorded human knowledge, what would that invention be? It would be the organization. Be it a private company, a nonprofit, or government establishment, each of these institutions have brought together individuals and teams to create what was once believed to be impossible through the 'organization'.

Because organizations are really nothing more than the combination of people and resources, the story of organizational change is really the story of people change. As demonstrated in each of the examples of

NASA, the World Health Organization, the National Human Genome Research Institute, and Alphabet (Google) above, when people come together with a common set of goals and shared purpose, and bring a collective commitment to executing against those goals and shared purpose, almost anything can be accomplished. By the same token, when people in the same organization under the umbrella of a common vision and purpose are not committed, it can be nearly impossible to accomplish even the most basic goals. Commitment to change is the linchpin that connects people to the purpose and goals of their organization.

Four Trends Changing Organizations and Work

We are living (and working) through extraordinary changes in work and organizational culture. The workplace landscape has been shifting dramatically over the past 5 to 10 years with the rise of social media, the changing nature of when and where work gets done, and even what it means to be an employee or worker. These changes are making the boundaries between work, personal time, and leisure less clear. At the same time, expectations of leaders have increased. Not only are they expected to be "agile" but they have to do more with less, meet higher productivity and quality standards, and "delight" customers- and most have to do so with smaller budgets. They are expected to engage and create cultures that meet the needs of their teams. On all sides, expectations are increasing. Here are a few trends shaping work.

Trend #1 – The Gig Workforce

There's a growing "gig" or freelance economy. Over the next few years, as much as 40% of the US workforce will be comprised of freelance workers.[6] Many organizations are executing and planning for "blended workforces" where freelance workers work alongside full-time employees to complete various projects. Marriott, Inc., for example, has a team that focuses exclusively on hiring contractors and temporary staff to more flexibly augment spikes in customer demand and support ongoing work needs. Entire portions of the tech sector are devoted to enabling this trend including Uber and Lyft in the transportation industry, Airbnb in the hotel and lodging industry, and Freelancer and Guru for professional services. A recent series of Uber commercials depict this trend best as it shows eager, fun-loving, protagonist Uber drivers transitioning from, "...earning to working to chilling".[7]

The freelance/gig economy trend suggests that many workers will increasingly expect, if not demand, more flexibility from their employers. As full-time employment opportunities become increasingly competitive, workers will begin to supplement part-time opportunities with smaller, limited scope, supplemental 'gig' opportunities. This will provide opportunities for leaders to create more engaging projects. Organizational leaders will need to 'sell change' across a broader range of worker types (internal and external) to drive the types of organizational outcomes they need to achieve.

Trend #2 – Social and Analytical Skills on the Rise

In addition to this trend, employment and wages have been disproportionately clustered in areas of the economy that require higher skills and greater levels of education. Pew research shows that employment is rising faster in jobs and occupations that require higher levels of education and people in jobs requiring higher levels of social (e.g., interpersonal, management, and communication) and analytical (e.g., critical thinking and technology) skills find that their wages are increasing.[8]

This trend indicates that moving into the future, any given organization's workforce will be comprised of better educated, more savvy, and astute individuals. Josh Bersin, the Founder of human capital consultancy, Bersin by Deloitte, put it well in a recent issue of Undercover Recruiter, "The jobs that are being created are actually jobs that focus on the essential human skills: listening, convincing, selling, communicating, designing and curating."[9] In this context, it will be increasingly difficult for leaders to hide or tell workers things that are misleading or wholly untrue. This trend also signifies the importance of organizational leadership skills such as emotional intelligence and social awareness. Leaders who are able to tap into the analytical capabilities of their teams and do so in ways that are emotionally engaging will differentiate their organizations as great places to work.

Trend #3 – Making Work an Experience

There is also a growing trend towards the "experience-ification" of work where workers gravitate towards workplaces, work experiences, and work cultures that will provide them with opportunities to gain meaningful experiences. In this new and emerging mode of work, workers will increasingly select and opt to remain at workplaces that keep them engaged emotionally, intellectually, physically, technologically, and culturally. Managers, human resources, and learning departments alike have begun focusing their energy on activities that will deliver employee experiences that use the latest digital technologies and will be personalized, compelling, and memorable for each worker.[10]

The net result of this trend is that organizations that creating meaningful work environments and engaging work experiences will "win" talent. People will want to work for these organizations because they know they will have the opportunity to do engaging work, work with a good manager and team, gain valuable experience

11

that can be leveraged on a resume for future work opportunities, and maybe even have fun while in the process. This need not mean foosball tables and free lunch everyday but the ability to create a work environment that is engaging, collaborative, and rallies people around purposeful, meaningful goals.

Trend #4 – Transparency & Rapid Transformation

The final trend is a dual trend towards the democratization of the workforce coupled with a more rapid need for change. What does this mean? There is an overall trend towards the workplace becoming more transparent, flexible, and open with a focus on allowing workers to express themselves and having an engaging work environment. This trend is exemplified by organizations that allow people to work flexible schedules and greater focus on work from home practices in organizations ranging from US federal agencies to the likes of Amazon, UnitedHealth, and Dell.[11] Tech firms such as Buffer, SumAll, and WholeFoods Market (now also Amazon) have made the salary information of their employees publicly available.[12] Workers are expecting greater levels of flexibility around when and how work gets done even while being "always on" and connected to work via email, and increasingly, text messages.

Organizational leaders are facing increased pressure to accelerate the pace of workplace changes needed to enable their organizations to remain nimble and meet growing budgetary and customer demands. This confluence of factors can prompt some leaders to get more creative and adaptable in their workplace approaches or it can cause some to double-down on more rigid leadership styles. Like Jacques Nasser, nicknamed "Jack the knife" for his cost-cutting efforts during his time at Ford, or Bob Nadelli who in his efforts to cut costs and bring a performance-focused culture to Home

Depot, ended up alienating employees.[13][14] The need for and the process of making the journey through large-scale transformation efforts can bring out the best or the worst in leaders and cultures. What we'll see in the following chapters is that leaders who have succeeded where other have failed are not shy about making difficult decisions that can result in major upheavals and even job losses, but they do so in a way that is transparent, engaging, and results-focused.

Together, these four trends represent a Dickensonian 'best-of-times-worst-of-times' era of work for organizational leaders looking for top talent and workers looking for their next opportunity to grow and acquire skills and experiences that will make them more marketable. At the same time, technology is enabling a more globally dispersed and "always connected" workforce through the "gig" economy. Hiring trends and wage practices indicate very talented workers have more options and opportunities for gainful employment and work. This will challenge organizational leaders to devise ever more creative ways of making work an engaging experience that will entice workers across the labor spectrum. Expectations are increasing on both sides as workers look to employers to provide meaningful and memorable work and employer organizations look for high-skilled, highly engaged talent to create leading services, exceptional products, and engaging customer interactions. Effective organizational change and transformation practices will need to factor-in all of these elements because as we move forward, workplace change will represent a flashpoint for leaders to engage with team members. Be it a merger, digital transformation, or customer-focused process improvements, organizational change will provide opportunities for workers to bring their best selves to work and make their mark—a strong factor of employee engagement. Organizational change will also be the opportunity for organizational leadership to demonstrate their ability to influence the organization and engage team members in meaningful ways that support successful organizational transformation.

When I Was Your Age...

The seeds of this new mode of work were being planted as I began my career in Human Resources (HR) nearly 15 years ago at a small, now defunct, HR outsourcing company in the suburbs of Columbus, OH. In the years since, I have consulted for leaders at massive, privately-held corporations, global fortune 500 companies, and US federal and state agencies who have been tasked with adapting their workforces and work processes to these new realities. Then, as now, workplace change has been a constant factor. Whether it was the boom that led to the dot-com bust, the shift towards large enterprise resource planning (ERP) systems, the rise of social media platforms, or the recent shift towards digital transformation, the landscape has changed dramatically for work and workers over the past 20 years. In a time when average worker tenure is decreasing and employee engagement is on the decline, change commitment functions as a way of binding workers to organizational goals and priorities.

When I first started this particular change journey I was really interested in what caused people to be committed to change taking place in the workplace, particularly in situations where workers were very concerned about losing their jobs. What, if anything, could possibly cause these individuals to still believe--to still be committed to changes in their organizations that they believed would likely result in them having to look for alternative employment opportunities? Through a series of interviews and surveys with over a thousand employees, plant managers and store managers alike, the answer to that question began to emerge. The key to highly engaged commitment to organizational change despite potential personal risks seems to lay in a combination of factors that include impact, influence, and consistency. Having devised detailed organizational change plans and led transformations throughout my career, over time I began to develop a nagging feeling that something was missing. Usually that feeling led me to dig even deeper into creating a better change plan, a more detailed communication strategy or some combination of the two. But the lived experience of witnessing people experience transformations for themselves and hearing them talk about it had much less to do with the technicalities of the particular change and much more to do with real-world impacts. Water cooler discussions I overheard in the hallways following big transformation-focused town hall meetings tended to focus less on the particulars of any change like the timeline or why the company was pursuing that particular path. Instead, conversations were focused on things like "will I have a job when this is over" or "this is going to make my job harder" or "the last time we tried this it didn't work so well" or "what are they *really* up to". These questions and comments are what I call the 'dinner table conversations of change'--those things that really matter and the aspects of the change process that people are much more likely to discuss over dinner with a spouse or close friend.

The key to highly engaged commitment to organizational change despite potential personal risks seemed to lay in a combination of factors that include impact, influence, and consistency.

Executives and HR/change managers like myself get really excited and fixated on timelines roadmaps and, one of my personal favorites, "future-state designs", but rarely are those the things that get the typical employee excited about, committed, or bought-in to a change initiative. This disconnect about change is supported by research showing that, following the announcement of several major change initiatives at a large, metropolitan hospital, rumors began to spread among various employees. The number one concern expressed by 776 survey respondents were around changes to their job and working conditions.[15] Findings like these seemed to align to my own experience as a change manager. Typical change management models focused on the type and nature of change but had a more limited focus on the types of things employees who were responsible for executing those changes were concerned about. It was my observations about this fundamental disconnect between organizational change management writ large and those dinner-table change discussions that got me thinking, what is it that really gets employees onboard with a new way of doing things?

Why Commitment Matters

This book is premised on the idea that when change leaders can get their teams committed to change in the workplace, the results will be improved change outcomes, better change execution, and more engaged teams. Leaders can drive this level of commitment by increasing the impact of change, facilitating influence, and creating consistency. These three factors of highly-engaged change commitment are supported by neuroscience research that outlines neurological decision-making processes and change management research, as well as real-world examples outlined in the following chapters. Increasingly, organizational leaders at all levels and their teams are being asked to change with greater levels of speed and precision than ever before. They will need every cognitive, emotional and behavioral resource available to them to ensure successful outcomes. While there will always be a place for foundational change management tools such as change plans, stakeholder communication plans, and impact assessments, the difference between successful and unsuccessful change results will come down to how well change leaders are able to drive commitment and engage their teams throughout each stage of change. As we move into the future, change leaders will need to position organizational transformations in ways that will create impact, build influence, and deliver consistency to generate adequate levels of commitment within their teams needed to achieve next-level performance and change success. This is doable when change leaders are able to sell change across their organization effectively.

Selling change is the approach leaders use to effectively communicate workplace changes in ways that boost team member commitment and buy-in to those changes.

Selling change is the approach leaders use to effectively communicate workplace changes in ways that boost team member commitment and buy-in to those changes. This includes talking about, discussing, and behaving in ways that lets team members understand the impact, importance, and worthwhile-ness of committing to and supporting change efforts. In other words, selling change communicates why this change matters and why others should buy-in to it (e.g., buy it). While the concept of sales may conjure images of less than trustworthy hucksters or a not-my-job response, the fact is that sales is nothing more than influencing others to commit to a particular course of action. Leaders who are able to drive change commitment more effectively will be more successful at delivering change within their organizations. Commitment to change represents a new way of thinking about organizational change in a way that puts the people who are responsible for executing workplace change at the heart of the change process--not simply as "change targets" but as responsible adults whose ideas and effort are invaluable to making change happen. At its core, organizational change is about the interplay between discretionary effort, momentum, and communication effectiveness. In most organizations, a new initiative can only achieve success if enough people are willing to put forth effort to support it. For instance, a new cloud-based software platform is only as effective at generating usable customer insights as team members' willingness to use it to store key sales or employee data. Cross-team collaboration following a merger is only as effective as team members' willingness to work together and share key work processes and customer information. New product designs are only as effective as those who are willing to contribute ideas and work collaboratively to transform an idea from design into a usable service or product. In each case, team members in the workplace have the power to accelerate or bring a major workplace transformation to a grinding halt depending on their overall willingness to engage with and commit to change.

Questioning the Change Process

The first question I ask anyone who is trying to implement change in their organization is: why would people commit to this change? If the majority of people on the team commit to changes taking place because they see the changes as meaningful, the leadership approach provides adequate information and influence, and there is an adequate level of trust, then the foundation is in place to build and carry-out a successful change program. The second question I ask is: how are you maintaining commitment? If the majority of people who are impacted by the change can see consistency to change being reinforced throughout the change process and there is a high degree of trust, then there's a high probability the change will be successful. How can I be so sure? The research on hundreds of successful organizational change projects bears this out. If we start by looking at change initiatives that were successful, then look backwards to examine what made them so, across industries, leaders, and change types the same themes appear again and again. Impact, influence, and consistency are the 'ingredients' that drive the highest levels of commitment to change in the workplace.

This book is for leaders who want to drive meaningful change in their organization. My goal is to help broaden your change management toolkit by pulling together the best insights from my own change management experience and research as well as psychology, neuroscience, and examples from successful, real-world changes. While all major organizational changes bring some degree of uncertainty and have the potential to trigger less-than-desirable emotional responses, *Selling Change* is about the things change leaders can do to position planned organizational changes in ways that get people to buy-in to those changes based on how the human brain processes information and makes decisions. Many popular change models aptly describe how to manage a change program-- e.g. creating a sense of urgency, creating a vision, building a guiding coalition, etc. but the goal of this book is not to build a better or more improved change management structure. Rather, my goal is to give change leaders a peek into the minds of those impacted by change to reveal what is happening at any given stage of the change process. Understanding what the change process looks like from the perspective of those who are impacted will help change leaders better tailor their change management approaches, messaging, and actions to increase the levels of commitment needed to ensure effective change outcomes.

The Selling Change Approach

The process of crafting and leading impactful and influential change approaches can be daunting, particularly when the objectives of your change initiative involve multiple stakeholders and perhaps even a negative history of unsuccessful transformation. This book was designed to provide a roadmap for thinking about what makes leading organizational change effective. As I collated the great research already done on the topic of organizational change along with my own change management experience and insights derived from leaders I have worked closely with, I've incorporated each of these elements into the chapters of this book.

Change in the Real World

Outside of the field, the value and usefulness of change management has been questioned and this is due in part to the fact that people-related change and transformation risks are either unknown or undervalued. The result is that people-focused change risks go unaddressed and contribute to the 60-70% of organizational change failures. This chapter delves into the statistics behind why organizational change and transformations fail. I unpack the infamous 70% change failure rate to show the specific types of organizational changes that fail and the factors that contribute most to those failure rates. To mitigate against these risks, a change risk calculation model is introduced to support change leaders in determining a change management budget for each of the different types of people-related risk factors. People analytics case studies are also included as well as a proven social science model that has successfully predicted behavior change across a range of change types and industries.

Faulty Change Assumptions

This chapter outlines three common faulty change management assumptions including a key ingredient missing from many of the most commonly used change management models. It also addresses the misconception that workers are naturally inclined to resist change and offers an alternative explanation rooted in real examples of how organizations, by simply modifying their change-focused messaging, significantly increased change commitment levels.

A Research Story (The Making of a Change Commitment Model)

This is the most personal of the book's chapters. It outlines the journey that led me to the research findings on organizational change commitment as well as the origins of the 2IsC™ Model based on insights derived from my research findings of over 650 workers in the manufacturing and retail industries. This chapter also addresses why change commitment is such an important element in the change leadership process. This is also the most research-focused chapter of the book detailing the factors that make up the 2IsC™ Model and how they correlate to highly engaged commitment to change. Not to fear, there are plenty of examples of how these concepts get brought to life in real organizational contexts. Packed with references to organizational and social science research, science-oriented practitioners and leaders can use this chapter to better understand the empirically-proven factors that drive effective change leadership.

Using Impact and Influence to Sell Change

This chapter is designed to bring the 2IsC(™) to life by providing practical steps change leaders can take to effectively communicate about and message change and transformation across multiple stakeholder groups. The tips and tools included in this chapter provide a sound basis for training and crafting change-focused communications for existing or your next change initiative. You will want to have this chapter open as you are crafting your next change communication email or planning the next change management workshop. Along the way, leader examples are included that demonstrate how these work in organizational settings making this one of the most usable chapters in the book.

2IsC™ (Impact, Influence, & Consistency) in Action

Having already explored the theoretical and empirical roots of Impact, Influence, and Consistency, this chapter pivots to focus exclusively on how leaders at real organizations with real-world workforce challenges, budgets, and constraints led their teams to organizational transformation success. Learning from others can help in navigating the change journey. Examples are taken from organizations in a cross-section of industries including Nissan, New York University Langone Medical Center, Box, Chipotle, and Build-A-Bear Workshop. In each case, the principles of Impact, Influence, and Consistency are highlighted for each step of the transformation journey to show what leaders in these organizations did to "sell change" to their teams and turn cross-team change commitment and buy-in into tangible organizational results.

Creating an Outcomes-Focused Change Strategy

Too often, change leaders get caught-up in the minutiae of organizational change such as creating the change plan or getting the communications "just right". While those elements are important, those are not typically the main focus of truly successful change leaders because they are instead focused on ensuring the right questions are being asked and answered in the minds of their team members. Once that has occurred, the work of "managing change" gets transferred away from only the change leader to each team member. This chapter outlines what each of those questions are and what leaders can do to ensure all team members are included throughout the change process while receiving the information and role-modeling needed to get them to buy-in and commit to workplace changes. The goal is to make change viral so that critical change mindsets, behaviors, and attitudes spread quickly throughout the organization. This chapter details how to make that happen.

Concluding Thoughts

The final chapter recapitulates the central themes and lessons throughout the book with a call-to-action for change leaders to think differently about change and transformation. Spoiler alert: Transformational change requires leaders to generate novel ideas and figure out ways to disseminate those ideas to multiple levels of the organization. In so doing, effective change leaders pave the way for multiple change types including digital transformation, agile, new product innovations, increased customer orientation, or whatever other change is needed to generate organizational growth and success.

Resources on the Selling Change Journey

As you read, you may find it helpful to understand your own levels of change commitment and commitment levels in your own organization. On our website, www.TheChangeShop.com, you can take a brief change commitment survey to better understand your commitment level and change leadership approach for changes occurring in your organization. You can also send a short **[Team Lead]180** or **[Change Lead]180** survey to your team, division, or entire organization to understand commitment levels across your organization. These tools will help you understand the areas of commitment and resistance in your organization and track how those levels change over time. The **[Personal]180** survey is free and only takes a few minutes to complete and rate to see your own levels of commitment to change in your workplace. Each can be particularly helpful to understand where your change commitment levels are as you read through the remainder of the book.

I will share additional insights and research on The Change Shop™ blog. If you have ideas or questions, or want to share stories of your own organizational change journeys, feel free to send an email to Robert@TheChangeShop.com.

Chapter 1 - Change in the Real World

"…with no data to validate the return on investment, change management doesn't attract the resources it requires…"

Michael Tushman & Anna Kahn

The field of change management is on the precipice of whole-sale change itself. In an era of big data and growing insights about human cognition, behavior and project management effectiveness, we now have more data than ever to evaluate what makes change work or not. I used to be skeptical of statistics showing that over 70% of organizational change initiatives fail.[16] Part of the skepticism had to do with how do you define "failure," since there are so many different types of organizational changes and since organizations often implement multiple changes simultaneously, how do you know when it has failed? Some change initiatives meet all, some, or none of their objectives. A change initiative that meets at least some objectives probably should not be classified as a "failure". One recent global change management study found that:

- 41% fully met objectives
- 44% missed at least one objective
- 15% missed all objectives or was aborted[17]

This puts that total percent of change projects "failing," at least partially, at closer to 60%. Semantics aside, if we define organizational change failure as a general lack of acceptance towards a new way of doing things, or a critical number of team members not adapting to new performance expectations, then the 60-70% figure seems reasonable. Most people think change failure is attributable to poor planning, not having enough resources, bad ideas, or unexpected 'bad luck' but as Scott Keller and Colin Price described in their book, *Beyond Performance*, a deeper look into the statistics of that infamous 70% change failure figure reveals that employee resistance to change and management behaviors that fail to support the change make up the vast majority of the causes of change failures. After seeing this figure, it becomes clear that most change failures are actually people failures. On the worker side, resistance to change indicates most did not think the change was worth committing themselves to (39%) and on the management side, leaders appear to inadequately support the changes in ways that increase workers' motivation to commit to change (33%). Change failure is both a top-down and bottom-up challenge. In some cases, it can be both, particularly when employees see managers or executives who are not supporting a particular course of action. Naturally, these team members will be less inclined to do so themselves. There is a cascading and ricocheting effect to change resistance.

Change Failures ARE People Failures

A 2017 study of over 2,000 business and IT leaders in 53 different countries found that lack of collaboration between different parts of the business was the number one reason digital transformation efforts stalled.[18] Technology and consulting firm IBM conducted a large-scale change management study that included interviews and surveys of over 1,500 change and project managers across 15 different countries and 21 industries across a range of projects and organizational changes with objectives that included: improving customer satisfaction, sales and revenue growth, cost reductions, process innovation, technology implementation, and new market entry. People factors were among the top three contributors to change failures

Key Barriers to Successful Change

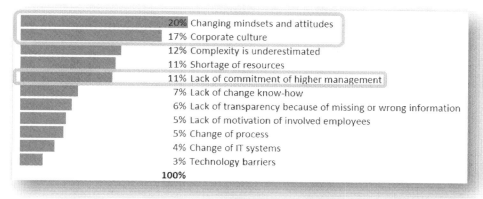

Figure 1. Barriers to Successful Change
Source: IBM, Inc. (2008) Making Change Work Study

The top 2 barriers were both people-related barriers and account for over a third of all factors contributing to change barriers. If we factor all people related barriers (e.g., lack of commitment, lack of change know-how, lack of motivation, etc.) that figure jumps to 65%, quite close to the 70% change failure figure many change researchers cite again and again. The reoccurring message seems to be the probability of organizational change failure is high and the reasons for those failures consistently point to people-related change risks.

Mitigating Change Risks (planning for and pricing real-world change)

In other any other business context, if leaders were able to, in advance, identify the number one risk factor to a new venture or large investment, they would develop a mitigation strategy to effectively address that risk. They would put a portion of their project budget towards ensuring the factors that could put the investment at risk were adequately addressed and accounted for before moving forward. The same should be true for organizational change. The numbers speak for themselves.

So how much should you spend to reduce change and transformational project risks? Risk management refers to the process of identifying and proactively responding to risks associated with introducing, leading, and managing change. In most cases, large change initiatives will have an associated budget. Change leaders and managers can better position themselves as effective leaders when they can both identify change risks in advance and quantify the monetary impacts of those risks. Since we know in advance that most change initiatives are only partially successful, contingency budgets can be used as a tool to gauge how much should be set aside to support effective change management efforts. Risk contingency budgets can be tapped so that budgets and expectations of executives don't become wildly misaligned when people-related issues inevitably arise during change projects. How much should you put towards risk contingency? You can use the Expected Monetary Value (EVM) as a method to quantify the risk in budgetary terms. EVM consists of two main components:

P – probability that the risk will occur
I – the impact to the change initiative if the risk occurs

By using these factors to assess the risks for your change projects, you can devote a portion of your change and/or project budget to mitigate change risks. For instance, say you have a $1MM change project. If you identify six risks to your change project based on the above 'Barriers to Successful Change', your risk contingency would look something like the following:

Risk	P (Risk Probability)	I (Cost Impact)	Risk Contingency (potential Change Mgmt. Budget)
Inability to change mindsets and attitudes across a critical mass of stakeholders	20%	$1,000,000	$200,000
Limited ability to shift culture to align to a new direction	17%	$1,000,000	$170,000
Lack of commitment from a critical number of senior managers	11%	$1,000,000	$110,000
Lack of motivation from impacted stakeholders	5%	$1,000,000	$50,000
		Total	$530,000

You might look up to see whether you might catch a glimpse of pigs flying if you see a change project spend of nearly half a million dollars on change management efforts for a $1MM investment opportunity, but if we are to take seriously the prospect that organizational change failures are primarily the result of people-related barriers, then we must invest accordingly. In the IBM study, organizations that invested less than 11% of the total project budget in change management had project success rates of nearly 35% while those organizations that invested more than 11% upped their project success rate to 43%.[19]

Real world Change Management Budgeting

The above chart should not be used in a literal way to project or estimate change management budgets. However, it is intended to illustrate the point that people-related risk factors should be considered significant project/investment risks and should be calculated accordingly when planning for large-scale change and transformation projects. According to one Gartner study, companies allocate an average of 5% of the total program/project budget to change management activities and that *includes* training.[20] They recommend allocating 15% of the project budget to change management support activities. To help change leaders in their planning efforts, the chart below provides a comparison of "low", "medium", and "high" change management spenders. The chart also provides a comparison to the contingency budget based on people-related change risks outlined above. This offers both a realistic view of change management spend alongside a view of much should be allocated if we are to take people-related change risks seriously. Taken together, this can be used to help guide decisions about how much should be allocated to support large-scale change/transformation initiatives. Specifically, the project contingency would be $530,000 for a $1MM project based on the presence of all five people-related change risks (e.g., $1MM*53%). However, based on more typical spending amounts as a portion of project totals, the change management contingency would be as follows:

Typical Spending Type	% Allocated to Change Management	Change Management Budget	Calculation
High Spenders	15%	$79,500	($1MM*15%)*53%
Moderate "Recommended" Spenders	11%	$58,300	($1MM*11%)*53%
Average "Typical" Spenders	5%	$26,500	($1MM*5%)*53%
Low Spenders	2.5%	$13,250	($1MM*2.5%)*53%

The following chart provides a more detailed breakdown showing change management allocations by each of the people-related change risks. Whereas the 53% risk probably assumes all people-related risks are present, this may not be the case for every organization so the more detailed view allows change leaders to see the actual and typical contingencies based on each risk type for a $1MM project.

Sample Change Management Budget Allocation Based on People-Related Risks

Overall Project Budget	Change Management Risk Type	Change Risk Probability	Contingency Based on Actual Change Management Risk	Contingency for Based on 3 "Typical" Change Management Spending Types			
				High Spenders (15%)	Moderate "Recommended" Spenders (11%)	Average "Typical" Spenders (5%)	Low Spenders (2.5%)
$1,000,000	Inability to change mindsets and attitudes across a critical mass of stakeholders	20%	$200,000	$30,000	$22,000	$10,000	$5,000
	Limited ability to shift culture to align to a new direction	17%	$170,000	$25,500	$18,700	$8,500	$4,250
	Lack of commitment from a critical number of senior managers	11%	$110,000	$16,500	$12,000	$5,500	$2,750
	Lack of motivation from impacted stakeholders	5%	$50,000	$7,500	$5,500	$2,500	$1,250
	Totals		$530,000	$79,500	$58,300	$26,500	$13,250

To calculate a change management budget for your next major project or initiative, check out the Change Management Budget calculator at www.thechangeshop.com/calculator.

Measuring Change Outcomes

Much has been made about the importance of using metrics to measure organizational culture and effective change management. While things like leadership, culture, and motivation can be difficult to measure for a host of reasons, one thing we can measure with a high degree of accuracy is whether a given organizational change is meeting expected outcomes. Team members are either using the new tool to track sales or they are not. The cloud-based SaaS solution is being used to store employee data or it's not. The leadership development program is resulting in a stronger pipeline of director-level leadership talent or it's not. These do not have to be soft and squishy "intangible" outcomes. It is possible to identify an outcome and measure a set of behaviors against those outcomes. The precursor to change outcomes are behaviors, the antecedent to behaviors are attitudes (e.g., mental, emotional commitment to change), and it all begins with leaders who are able to effectively communicate the need for change.

Predicting Change-Related Behaviors

As any social scientist will lament, it is extremely difficult to consistently predict human behavior. What causes one individual or group to commit and do something on one day versus that same individual or group to resist on a different day? There is a seemingly limitless number of factors that can influence individual and group behavior and decision making. One bright spot in social sciences is research predicting technology usage behavior. When changes are introduced such as a new technology or software designed to support work processes, we can predict with a greater degree of certainty than ever the factors that will contribute to successful adoption. A model that has proven particularly effective in predicting actual behavior is the unified theory of technology acceptance and use of technology (UTAUT). This model has been used to successfully predict, over time, real-world behavior of surgeons' adoption of robot-assisted surgery in the healthcare industry, use of web-based video rather than face-to-face meetings for product development entertainment industry, use of industry databases to support sales in the telecom industry, and use of accounting software in the public service sector 1-month, 3-months, and 6-months after introduction and training.[21] A longitudinal study found that UTAUT accounted for 70% of the variance in behavioral intention to use and 50% of actual use.[22] Four constructions were found to consistently account for behavioral change: 1) performance expectancy, 2) effort expectancy, 3) social influence, and 4) facilitating conditions.

Factor	Definition	Similar to...
Performance Expectancy	Degree to which team members believe using the system will help her/him improve job performance	Change Impact (see The Impact Factor)
Effort Expectancy	Degree to which team members believe using the system (or change) is simple, easy or user-friendly	Influence (see Influence Factors)
Social Influence	Degree to which team members believe people who are important to them believe they should use the system	Leadership (see Change Influence factor #3: Why You?) Influence (see Using Impact and Influence to Sell Change)
Facilitating Conditions	Degree to which team members believe organizational and technical support is in place to support using the system	Consistency (see Consistency Factors)

These four factors can serve as a baseline for thinking about how organizational change is structured. Too often, organizational change is structured around communication and awareness--have we communicated enough? do the right stakeholders know about this effort?—but less focus is placed on the other key factors which show direct and consistent linkages to behavior change in organizational change contexts (e.g., performance and effort expectancy, social influence, and facilitating conditions). Only after organizational change is measured along outcome-based dimensions will the true value of organizational change data be realized.

Case Study: Predicting (and reducing) Turnover at McGraw Hill Financial

In much the same way banks use predictive analytics to determine the likelihood of loan recipients' ability to pay back loans, realtors use Google search data to predict housing market price changes, and retailers can combine demographic and weather data to predict sales and merchandising plans, so too can change management, talent, and human resources practitioners combine talent data to predict turnover and commitment levels to organizational changes.

Organizational leaders who make the commitment to invest in analytics are starting to see the benefits and this does not only apply to large tech giants like Alphabet (Google). At McGraw Hill Financial, HR and talent practitioners can pull "flight risk" information based on the profile of team members who are most likely to leave the organization in the near future by referencing characteristics such as gender, age, department, education, or skill/specialization. Using that information, the HR/talent team can decide whether to intervene to prevent potential unwanted turnover through a host of interventions including career/job moves or compensation adjustments. According to Mark Sullivan, Vice President HR Insights and Analytics, "This is one of the tools at our disposal which we didn't have a year or two ago." Often, young talent is looking for the next opportunity to grow their skills and make a mark. By linking change initiatives to high-turnover risk populations, there may be opportunities to hang on to talent by targeting them for inclusion in key change initiatives.[23]

A recent Center for American Progress study found that the cost to replace a typical employee is about 20% of the individual's salary.[24] For a department of 100 people who earn an average of $40,000, reducing turnover 10%, from 25% to 15%, translates into $80,000 in cost savings. Selling change in ways that reduce turnover translates into real value over time.

Bringing it all together

For years, the people side of large scale change and transformation initiatives has been underfunded and underserved so it must be no small wonder that the statistics seem to consistently show that 60-70% of change initiatives fail to deliver the expected results. That said, there are promising change management solutions and approaches that, if adopted, can significantly improve change initiative outcomes. It starts with diagnosing the real reasons behind change failures—people. When people are not committed to supporting proposed changes, the initiative will die on the proverbial vine. If people are the main causes of change failures, then organizational leaders need to plan their projects and change budgets around the people-related risks, including (in order of risk likelihood):

1. Inability to change mindsets and attitudes across a critical mass of stakeholders
2. Limited ability to shift culture to align to a new direction
3. Lack of commitment from a critical number of senior managers
4. Lack of motivation from impacted stakeholders

Across a range of change types and industries, these 4 people-related change risks have been shown to consistently lead to change failure.

Despite these risks and high rates of change failure, opportunities to address these risks are available. Reducing change risks involves proactively addressing people-related risks using several approaches, including:

Managing Change Risks: budgeting projects according to more accurate, research-based estimates of people-related risks.

Unified Theory of Acceptance and Use of Technology Model (UTAUT): by applying the principles from the UTAUT to the change management process, change leaders can leverage some of the best scientifically-proven, real-world-tested models for getting people to change their behavior.

Predictive Change Analytics: big data is a growing trend that can now be applied to predicting change and transformation outcomes. Tools for change leaders to do this are available at TheChangeShop.com.

Selling Change approach: selling change is about influencing team members in ways that will get them to want to commit to organizational changes. The more (and better) skilled organizational leaders are at selling change, the more effectively team members, teams, and organizations will change.

Effectively managing change is one of the most important activities leaders will undertake. The opportunities when change is successfully managed and led are tremendous, while the risks associated with failure are extremely high. When change leaders lack adequate or accurate change and people-related insights, their organizations run the risk of change failure which can have negative reverberating effects across future changes (e.g., team members who are less willing to take future change risks) in addition to financial and budgetary risks. With the right data and information on team members and their commitment levels, change leaders can shift the odds of successful transformation in their favor. The next chapter addresses risks inherent to several commonly used organizational change models. While every change model has its strengths, many fail to adequately account for factors such as commitment and buy-in, which are critical factors for overcoming change barriers.

Chapter 2 - Faulty Change Assumptions

"We did everything right, now I'm on the outside"

Calvin Harris and Elle Goulding

"We did everything right, so why are we getting so much pushback?" These were the words the Vice President of HR at a large, global technology client uttered to me in exasperated frustration during one of our change progress status meetings. Her frustration was palpable and other than a few platitudes and suggestions about ways we could provide additional workforce communications for the new shared service organization we were tasked with building, I did not have any good answers for her. In the years since, I have often thought about that meeting and all the work we put into standing up the new organization. She was right, we had done everything right, we had identified all the stakeholders across the organization, we had crafted and delivered targeted communications for each level and we had articulated the case for change and outlined, to an adequate level of detail, all the things that needed to change. We had done change management by-the-book and we were left with a workforce that was, at its core, unwilling to commit to making the new organizational structure successful in any way other than begrudgingly. In hindsight, it occurred to me the reason was the change management playbook itself.

I have become increasingly convinced there are three common assumptions that prevent transformational changes from achieving their full potential. I learned this the hard way as a change lead in sunny, southern California. It is possible to have an organizational change that produces successful outcomes and even results in a transformed organization or workplace, but if organizational leaders fail to garner a critical mass of commitment, the overall change is at risk of limited support, inadequate buy-in, and limited behavioral change once the change has been implemented. In the following sections, we explore three faulty change management assumptions leaders and change practitioners make when planning, executing, and deploying change and transformation initiatives in their workplaces. Some of these you may agree with and others you may not, but if you are operating under all three, then your change initiative runs a significantly increased risk of change failure.

Faulty Assumption #1: Change Management Models Account for Change Commitment

Most change leaders use some type of model or framework when attempting to guide the change management process. Common organizational change models include John Kotter's 8-step model, the Organizational Change Management framework, the SCARF (status, certainty, autonomy, relatedness, and fairness) Model, and the ADKAR (awareness, desire, knowledge, ability, and reinforcement) Model. What follows is a brief outline of each of these models. These models will be familiar to many change managers and practitioners, however, closer examination reveals something interesting and missing—none of these models account for ways to drive team member commitment. Let's begin.

The Kotter Model

I start with this one because it is one of the most popular and widely-used organizational change management models in the world. This model was devised by John P. Kotter, a Harvard Business School Professor and author of several books on change management. Each of the 8-steps address a key principle that is associated with people's responses to change.

Kotter's 8 steps

- **Increase urgency** – This step involves creating a sense of urgency among the people so as to motivate them to move forward towards objectives.

- **Build the team** – This step of Kotter's change management theory is associated with getting the right people on the team by selecting a mix of skills, knowledge, and commitment.
- **Get the vision correct** – This stage is related to creating the correct vision by taking into account not just the strategy, but also creativity, emotional connect, and objectives.
- **Communicate** – Communication with people regarding change and its need is also an important part of the change management theory by Kotter.
- **Get things moving** – In order to get things moving or empower action, remove the roadblocks and implement feedback in a constructive way.
- **Focus on short term goals** – Focusing on short term goals and dividing the ultimate goal into small and achievable parts is a good way to achieve success without too much pressure.
- **Don't give up** – Persistence is the key to success, and it is important not to give up while the process of change management is going on, no matter how tough things may seem.
- **Incorporate change** – Besides managing change effectively, it is also important to reinforce it and make it a part of the workplace culture.[25]

With its basis in real-world change management research and strong, intuitive, momentum-building flow, there is little doubt about why the Kotter model is one of the leading change management models on the planet.

The Organizational Change Management framework

The next model is the Organizational Change Management (OCM) framework. This particular model is especially near and dear to me personally because it was the one most commonly used for executing enterprise-wide change management projects during my time at Accenture. Overall, this tool states there are five steps stakeholders pass through throughout the change process, including: unawareness, awareness, understanding, acceptance, and commitment.

OCM's 5 Stages

- **Unawareness:** Stakeholders do not know that change is going to happen.
- **Awareness:** Stakeholders know that change is imminent. They don't know yet what will be the benefits coming from the change.
- **Understanding:** Stakeholders can explain the impact of the change on them and on their organization.
- **Acceptance:** Stakeholders have a positive attitude towards the change and of the changes that will affect them. They are willing to "give it a try."
- **Commitment:** Stakeholders will champion the changes associated with the change to their peers and will do everything in their power to make it work and deliver the expected benefits in their organization.

Because this particular model is commonly applied across multiple target groups (e.g., the project team, project sponsors, managers, employees, et al.) and allows change managers to easily track communications and training across each of these groups, it is particularly useful when applied to large-scale transformation efforts where multiple stakeholders are involved.

The ADKAR Model

The ADKAR Model is an individual level focused model that outlines the journey team members go through during the change process. ADKAR is an acronym that stands for awareness, desire, knowledge, ability, and reinforcement.[26] This process describes what the model creators call the "people side" of change management.

ADKAR's 5 Stages of People Change

- Awareness of the need for change
- Desire to support and participate in the change
- Knowledge of how to change
- Ability to implement required skills and behaviors
- Reinforcement to sustain the change

As with the other change models, the usefulness of the ADKAR model is difficult to dispute and it is both intuitive and practical in terms of the ability to follow the natural progression from becoming aware of the need for change through supporting change once it has been implemented.

The SCARF Model

One of the more recent change models is the SCARF® model.[27] With its basis in neuroscience research showing that problem-solving capacity is increased when individuals collaborate and that same capacity is reduced under conditions of threat, the SCARF model takes a decidedly 'social' approach to bringing people together when managing change. SCARF stands for status, certainty, autonomy, relatedness, and fairness and is summarized in the following five steps:

- Status is about relative importance to others.
- Certainty concerns being able to predict the future.
- Autonomy provides a sense of control over events.
- Relatedness is a sense of safety with others - of friend rather than foe.
- Fairness is a perception of fair exchanges between people.

In comparison to the other 4 models, SCARF places social needs and threat reduction at the core of the change management process. The model is ideal for change circumstances where high levels of collaboration and teamwork are required to ensure the change can be brought to fruition.

So what's missing?

With this summary review of five commonly used change management models, there is little doubt about why these are so frequently used by change practitioners. Each has clear strengths and can be applied to multiple change scenarios. That said, each of these models miss the critical commitment factor. The ADKAR model has the 'desire' step, but again, this presumes that the desire for the change is either already present or needs to be generated but it does not outline the steps needed to create change desire.

The OCM model has a step called commitment, that step refers to how team members will behave once they have already made a decision to commit to the change. It does not address how to create or increase commitment. In fact, as can be seen in Figure 2, even though the final stage of the OCM model is called 'Commitment/ Ownership' the fact is commitment decisions are made at multiple stages prior, including between **1)** Awareness and Understanding, **2)** Understanding and Acceptance, and **3)** Acceptance and Commitment / Ownership.

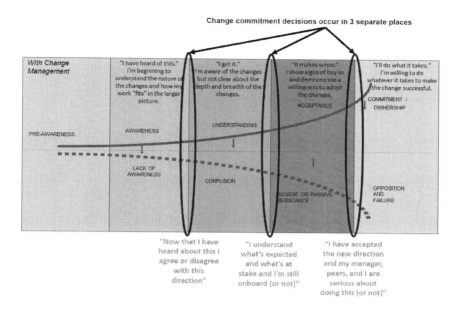

Figure 2. Change Commitment in the Organizational
Change Management Model

Commitment decision #1: After first hearing about a change, team members will make a decision about whether or not they think the change is a good or useful thing to do.

Commitment decision #2: After gaining a better understanding of the future and day-to-day impacts of the proposed changes, team members will make decisions about whether those are acceptable to them personally or organizationally.

Commitment decision #3: After accepting what may be, in many cases, 'the inevitable', individual team members will make a final decision about whether to commit whole-heartedly or half-heartedly to the new ways of doing things.

Additionally, these decisions are not made in an isolated way. More often than not, following the announcement of any major change initiative, chatter begins and the rumor mill starts, which also serves to frame whether and how change commitment decisions are made. What may seem to be on the surface a simple decision about committing to a future organizational direction, is in reality, a more complex and multi-phased decision-making process. Change management models that account for these complexities will enable leaders to more effectively communicate about needed changes at the right times and in the best ways possible. In chapter 3, I outline a research-based model specifically designed to create highly-engaged commitment in each change phase.

Faulty Assumption #2: Change Approaches Adequately Address Stakeholder Needs

One of the main reasons team members resist workplace change is because changes are perceived to threaten one or more of their fundamental individual needs. For example, transitioning to a flat or matrixed organization structure will threaten self-fulfillment needs by making it more difficult to get a long-worked-for promotion. Likewise, it is extremely difficult to get team members "onboard" with a change that is likely to have a negative impact on their financial, personal, or social well-being. Change leaders and implementers often introduce changes that threaten these needs without adequately accounting for ways reducing these core workforce needs will also reduce change commitment.

Abraham Maslow's hierarchy of needs theorized that once people had their basic needs met for things such as food, water, security, and safety, the next level of psychological needs (e.g., relationships, a sense of achievement) would be triggered. Once basic and psychological needs are met, individuals look to meet needs for self-fulfillment including creative activities.[28] One of the reasons managing the workforce transitions is so difficult is because each stage of the needs hierarchy is at play at any given time. People work to receive pay to meet their basic needs but the workplace is also a place where relationships are formed and people interact closely with each other, oftentimes more than with their own families, so psychological needs are also in play. Work is also a place where many seek to fulfill their self-fulfillment needs such as need for achievement. Whether moving up the proverbial corporate ladder or attempting to create the next great product, status and achievement are an important part of many people's "why" for going to work. Change in workplace carries the potential to threaten any one of these needs. The chart below outlines several factors to 'watch out' for during the change planning and implementation process. Ideally, a change impact assessment will be conducted prior to executing the change to better account for these psychological change risks, but if that is not possible, change leaders should setup discussions with key stakeholders or their managers to ensure key change needs are accounted for prior to, during, and after the transformation effort is complete.

Level	Need by Level	Need	Examples
5	Self-Actualization	Achievement	Autonomy, mastery, subject matter expertise
4	Esteem	Respect and Recognition	Perks, job titles
3	Belonging	Social and Relationships	Cooperative peers, good manager, best friend at work
2	Security	Work Environment	Benefits, workplace safety, working conditions, harassment/bully-free workplace
1	Physiological	Work Exchange	Pay/salary, stable employment, job security

Figure 3. Maslow's Hierarchy of needs applied to the Workforce

At the electronics client where I was leading the organizational redesign effort, our accelerated timeline limited our ability to conduct an impact assessment to determine whether people would be committed to the organizational changes we were attempting to implement. Had we completed an impact assessment even with only the managers, we might have uncovered various basic, psychological, or self-fulfillment needs that we might have been able to address upfront to pre-emptively improve commitment levels.

Faulty Assumption #3: Workers Naturally Resist Change

The final faulty assumption has to do with the way decision makers (executives/leaders) and decision executors (staff) think about and talk about the need for change. More often than not, change in organizations is top-down. This is not to say there are not occasions where the proverbial suggestion box feedback makes it to the top and a bottom-up change process gets championed, or that there are no organizations like Zappos with its flat organizational structure and hyper-focus on group decision-making, but overall, large-scale transformations come from the top and often get cascaded downward. This is the way organizations function—an individual or group at the top assesses the landscape and provides vision, direction, and guidance to a larger group of "doers," or team members who execute that direction.

Before a major transformation or change decision is made, organizational leaders often undergo a robust period of vetting alternatives, weighing different courses of action, and eventually coming to a decision on how best to proceed. In short, they go through their own version of a change commitment process. The end result of this process may result in success or failure, and it's often impossible to know the result of the decision until after sufficient time has passed, but in all but the most aggressive organizations, some version of this process is followed before a major change decision is made. Because team members who are impacted by change decisions are often not involved in the change-focused decision-making process and therefore not given the opportunity to similarly weigh the possible pros and cons, the final decision may seem nonsensical or incomprehensible to them. This can in-turn cause team members to resist change sometimes quietly or other times openly and quite visibly. This 'resistance' often happens because communication research demonstrates that people make sense of new and uncertain events by comparing the new situation to previous circumstances.[29] For instance, union workers may be asked to ratify a new contract that includes cuts to wages and benefits. Naturally, the union workers' first response is to compare the new proposed contract to the current contract. After seeing any reduction in benefits, they will almost invariably respond negatively. The executives who proposed the contract changes may attempt to defend the proposed contract, citing the cuts were not as extensive as they could have been, thus leading to an impasse. This is an example of one of the possible disconnects that often happens when change decisions are made and communicated. Both sides feel justified in their positions—managers feeling as though the cuts could have been much worse and union workers believing they are expected to work harder for even less. In this scenario, rather than simply allowing the union workers to compare the old contract to the proposed contract, providing them with a comparison framework might help to make the decision-making process more understandable and reduce resistance. For example, providing wage/benefit offerings to organizational performance five years

---

Resistance-proof Change Stories

A large US-based financial services company initiated a cost reduction program and leaders kicked-off the program with a "good to great" story. This story went as follows: "Our historical advantage has been eroded by intense competition and changing customer needs; if we change, we can regain our leadership position" and a turnaround story: "We're performing below industry standard and must change dramatically to survive. We can become a top-quartile performer in our industry by exploiting our current assets and earning the right to grow." Both stories had strong executive/management-focused themes but employee resistance remained a frustrating factor three months into the change effort.

The change team worked to modify the change story to one that included elements related to society (to deliver affordable housing), customers (fewer errors, more competitive prices), the company (expenses are growing faster than revenues, which is not sustainable), working teams (less duplication, more delegation), and individuals (more attractive jobs).

The result? This relatively simple shift in messaging lifted employee motivation scores from 35.4 percent to 57.1 percent in just one month, and the program went on to achieve 10 percent efficiency improvements in the first year—a run rate that exceeded initial expectations.

ago compared to current conditions would provide additional context needed to help workers better understand the context in which the reduction decision was made. This is an example of an information-based change leadership strategy which we will explore further in chapter 4.

Research shows that approximately 80% of what leaders communicate when introducing change initiatives fails to tap into 80% of what actually gets employees motivated to change. When talking about the need for change, leaders often make the mistake of overemphasizing the aspects of change that are important for the well-being and success of the organization while underemphasizing the aspects of the change process that are important for employees, society, and customers. Increasingly, societal benefit is one of the messaging levers that is of particular importance especially to the newest, largest segment of the workforce--millennials. This group in particular is interested in ways their organization (and by extension major changes in the organization) will have positive benefits for the wider society.[30] 71% of millennials believe business should do more to improve living standards, which is consistent with the top-most impact described below.

The goal in overcoming the executive/manager/employee divide in change communications is to communicate honestly yet frame change-related announcements in ways that all groups care about. When change impact factors for managers and employees were compared the following were the top impact areas both groups cared about equally and should serve as the basis for creating more effective and influential change communications:

- **Society / Purpose:** building the community and stewarding resources
- **Customer / Constituents**: providing superior service
- **Company / Organization:** financial health and shareholder returns
- **Working team:** creating a caring and trusting workplace

- **Individuals:** impact on "me" personally e.g., my development, paycheck, and bonus[31]

A faulty assumption exists that employees are often naturally resistant to change but the research shows that often, employees and managers are more aligned than both groups probably realize. Managers and employees alike care about customers, shareholders, and their organization's impact on society. When the need for change is framed in ways that address employee and manager concerns about impact, change commitment increases.

Bringing it all together

Throughout this chapter, we examined three faulty change assumptions change leaders (and the change models they sometimes use) make about the change process. These faulty assumptions result in less than expected team member commitment and can serve to undermine otherwise well-executed change management plans. The first assumption is that many widely-used change management models account for the role of workers' commitment throughout the change management process. The result, as I discovered during a client engagement with a global electronics client, is that change leaders, sponsors, and project teams can follow all of the correct steps to execute a well-designed change program only to find that a critical mass of team members remain uncommitted and fail to buy-in to the change effort. One solution for overcoming this is to measure change commitment and engagement levels throughout the change journey to gauge overall commitment levels and where "commitment risks" may be occurring.

The second faulty change assumption is that change approaches adequately account for the needs of impacted stakeholders. With the exception of aspects of the SCARF® Model, most change models and approaches do not account for the basic, psychological, or self-fulfillment needs of individuals impacted by organizational change. The result is that team members become resistant to change efforts not because they disagree with the intent or objectives of the change itself, but rather because they believe the change will negatively impact one or more of their need areas. One way to account for need-based "threats" during the change process is to conduct an impact assessment by setting up a brief survey, or a series of virtual lunch chats, or asking managers of impacted teams which areas are likely to be put at risk if the change moves forward as planned. Of course, these discussions are only useful in high-trust environments where people feel comfortable expressing their ideas and challenges.

The final faulty change assumption is that workers are naturally resistant to change. When compared to managers, workers tend to agree with managers on the importance of using organizational resources wisely (reduce waste), enhancing the customer or client experience (improve/increase customer satisfaction, retention and revenue), and creating a work environment that is positive (collaborative culture). From an intentionality perspective, the vast majority of organizational changes fall into one or more of these categories, which means that for nearly any proposed change initiative, executives, managers, and workers are inclined to agree that a change is needed and are generally aligned on the intention behind why the change is being proposed. In this context, the goal of change leaders is to frame the change in a way that is both transparent and honest yet also taps into the aspects of the change that are likely to engage all stakeholders. This is best done through story telling as demonstrated in the case of the financial services organization (see Resistance Proof Change Stories). Rather than talking about how a proposed change will improve the organization's performance or "bottom line," tell a story that taps into factors that will motivate the team—the impact the proposed change will have on society, customers, the organization, working teams, and individuals.

Chapter 3 - A Research Story (The Making of a Change Commitment Model)

"Our moods infuse our judgements. We are not cool computing machines; we are emotional creatures"

David Myers, Social Psychologist

"There is nothing so practical as a good theory."

Kurt Lewin, Father of Organization Development

The year was 2006 and summer was beginning to bleed into fall. Fresh out of the master's program in Human Resources and Labor Studies, I was just beginning the doctoral program in Organizational Leadership and Policy Development at the University of Minnesota. I had heard the horror stories of students who began their dissertations but never finished and I was resolutely determined not to become one of those people. So, by day, working as an internal Organization Development (OD) at Carlson Companies, Inc. (the parent company of renowned brands such as Country Inns & Suites, Radisson brand hotels, and the beloved TGI Fridays) and a doctoral student by night, I set myself to the task of completing the required dissertation coursework. My courses covered a range of topics from the history of work, to the use of technology in healthcare, to advanced OD, change management practices in developing countries, and macro organization behavior and theory. Along the way, I reviewed leading theories and thinkers in the field of change management and presented two conference papers on a couple of my favorite theories and how they could be applied in real-world settings.

As I matriculated through the program I grew increasingly interested in the topic of commitment to change and the role it plays in the change management process. One study I found particularly compelling was research comparing 3 different types of commitment to change including people who committed themselves to a change at work because they had to (e.g., "do it or else"), because they felt obligated to do so (e.g., "you owe us this"), and because they actually believed in the change and wanted to commit to it (e.g., "I want to do this").[32] The study was aptly titled, *Want To, Need To, Have To: Employee commitment to organizational change*. Though a bit unsurprising, the study found that individuals who fell into the "want to" form of commitment demonstrated higher levels of performance. They were also more willing to learn new skills and behaviors but, most importantly, their organizations showed higher rates of change implementation success. It seemed that affective commitment to change or "want to" commitment was the key to achieving successful change outcomes. After consulting with colleagues in my department and my dissertation committee members, I eventually settled on an approach I believed would be the mother of all change management research. I wanted to know if (and how) people could demonstrate "want to" levels of commitment to organizational changes even when those changes could be detrimental to them. In other words, how do you get people to commit to changes that would likely result in personally damaging outcomes. To test this, I used job loss risk as the outcome. Using a survey comprised of 88 questions and over ten different validated survey constructs, I was essentially asking people to tell me, would a pending change at work result in the loss of your job and, if so, are you still committed to doing what it takes to make that change a reality? I considered this the "holy grail" of change management - figuring out how to get people to commit to organizational changes that could result in the worst possible outcome for them personally—the loss of a job. Indeed, this represented the very bottom and most foundational part of Maslow's hierarchy. If there was a way to figure out what could make people commit to workplace changes such as these, then we would have cracked the code of effective change management. The theory was that practically any workplace change that would have less of an impact (than job loss) should be relatively easier to commit to by comparison.

Excited, I wrote-up my proposed study approach and presented it to my distinguished committee of professors. As I presented, the overriding feeling in the room was one of keen interest. The tone was very conversational and the committee asked about a range of questions and topics from where the idea for the study came from to NAFTA (North American Free Trade Agreement) due to the job loss implications. One of my committee members even told me she went to school with one of the creators of one of the job insecurity scales I proposed to use. The committee approved my research proposal and following an Internal Review Board (IRB) -- the group responsible for ensuring research is conducted ethically and will not result in harm to research subjects--everything seemed to be progressing swimmingly. Then it happened--my dissertation hit a brick wall.

A Time of Silence

First, I reached out to my LinkedIn contacts. The people in my immediate circle whom I had worked with and knew me were kind but offered excuses about poor timing or the study not being a great fit for their organization. A few people were interested but after reviewing the question set wanted to make too many changes that would fundamentally alter the survey items I would need to test my research hypotheses. I tried putting more and more marketing messages on LinkedIn and even physically mailed research one-pagers to business lists I found on Dunn and Bradstreet databases, but there were no takers. The year was now 2009 and, despite a couple of leads that ultimately went nowhere, my prized research project was all dressed up with nowhere to go. With each passing year, I was moving closer and closer to becoming one of those people who started, but never finished, their dissertation. I would become a dreaded 'ABD-er' (all but dissertation). The thought of that filled me with apprehension. At times, I was tempted to scale-back the dissertation proposal or perhaps turn it into something that did not require real-world survey respondents and I could pull similar information from an existing dataset. After all, at least that way it would be done. But each time that thought crossed my mind, I quickly dismissed it. As much as I wanted to have a completed dissertation, I knew becoming an academician was not a career goal for me so this was my one shot to make a meaningful contribution to scientific research. Additionally, I firmly believed in my research and was convinced that my approach was the best way to capture and test real people's perspective on change in their workplace and its impacts. So, month after month, year after year, I waited until the right organization came along.

One night in the spring of 2011 I happened to be at dinner with a family friend and the topic of a pending big process change came up. He told me the manufacturing company he worked for was about to roll out new processes that would threaten jobs and potentially make it easier to outsource work overseas. I listened excitedly knowing this was the perfect setting for my study but I kept telling myself this sounded too good to be true. After years of waiting there was simply no way the leadership at this company would allow me to survey their employees about such a sensitive subject matter during such a critical period. A week went by and the friend sent me the contact information for one of the company's HR Directors who oversaw employees across multiple states in the Midwest and Southeast US. I spoke to him and after a pleasant introductory conversation, he invited me out to the regional headquarters to meet with him and two other company executives. At the time, I was working on a project at a client based in New Mexico and instead of flying back to my then home in New Jersey, I booked a one-day layover in Baltimore, Maryland. That Friday morning, I was cautiously optimistic as I drove in to their building outside of Baltimore, but after having been turned down so many times before I thought surely as soon as the company leaders saw the survey questions they would change their minds and politely send me packing. The HR director, a plant manager, corporate director, and I were seated around a large conference room table and

I waited silently yet eagerly while the plant manager reviewed the survey questions. After what seemed like a short eternity, the plant manager looked up from the form and smiled, saying, "Let's move forward!" I was in a momentary state of disbelief. With a straight face, I asked if he was sure and he confirmed he wanted to move forward and in fact believed the information would be "very useful for the company".

About a month later, after distributing both web-based and paper-based versions of the survey to over 500 employees across the company's operations I was back in the same conference room presenting the company's location-specific results to a group of managers. For dissertation purposes, I had more than enough manufacturing industry information to have a statistically representative sample to test each of my research hypotheses. A year later I was able to obtain a similar sample from a large, nationwide retail company and complete the study I had planned for and proposed nearly three years earlier. I had finally managed to collect enough data to analyze and finish my dissertation.[33]

The Findings

The goal of the research was to find factors that contributed to what researchers call affective commitment to change ("want to" change) among workers when the change was likely to result in the loss of their jobs. The research also measured factors that contributed to three types of resistance to change. The three resistance types included emotional (e.g., I'm resisting this change because I don't feel good about), cognitive (e.g., I don't think it's a good idea), and behavioral (e.g., I already have or intend to do something to demonstrate my displeasure with this change). A summary of the factors are presented in Figure 4. Across 650 survey respondents, change impact showed the highest positive correlation with affective commitment to change or "want to"-style change, followed by perceptions of information-based change leadership strategy and trust in management. This finding forms the basis of the 2IsC™

Model. The summary version of this research-based model says that when individuals perceive organizational changes to be highly impactful, those changes are communicated in an informative way, they are given opportunities to participate in the change, and there are high levels of trust in management, then people will actually "want to" commit to change and will be emotionally invested in the change process. This held true even for highly job insecure people who believed the change was likely to result in the loss of their job and was true no matter the stage of the change (beginning, middle, or end). If those factors are present, people will commit to transformational changes at work. This is the proverbial "holy grail" of change management.

Making Sense of It All

On one hand, the findings seem to make intuitive sense. After all, people need to be convinced that workplace changes will matter to themselves personally or to the organization overall or both. It is very difficult to commit to a change happening at work if it seems insignificant or inconsequential. From the perspective of how change is managed, the results showed that workers who perceived leaders were using an information-based change leadership strategy was the second biggest predictor of highly engaged change commitment. In fact, for this cross-industry, cross-regional sample, an information-based change

> **Information vs Participation-based Change Leadership, Does It Matter?**
>
> A recent study compared the emotional, mental, and behavioral responses of U.S. county government workers towards implementation of a new, web-based performance management system. Performance management is always a challenging topic and difficult to "get right". The study found no statistical difference between workers who perceived leaders using an information-based vs. a participation-based change leadership approach. The findings further highlight the importance of being able to articulate the importance and impact of key organizational changes particularly when more participatory change management approaches are not feasible.

leadership approach was slightly more predictive than participation-based change leadership. This was one of the more surprising study findings. Much of the organizational change management literature suggests that participation is the most optimal way to get people committed to the change process but my research found that people seemed to prefer information when it came to how their workplace changes were managed. Although slight, the research showed that data, facts, and logic appeared to rule the day for people experiencing workplace change. Other researchers have uncovered similar results indicating adequate, relevant, and timely information about workplace change was one of the biggest contributing factors to workers' openness to change.[34,35] It was particularly interesting in my research to find that information-based change approaches still showed the biggest contribution to highly engaged commitment even when those changes carried the potential to threaten their jobs. Armed with information and a sense that management was being transparent and trustworthy, workers demonstrated a willingness to move forward despite the worst possible personal workplace outcome.

Two Eyes See (2IsC™)

As I began thinking about ways to frame this model, three words seemed to best encapsulate the true meaning of all the factors that contribute to highly engaged change commitment. These were impact, influence, and consistency. The two "Is" stand for impact and influence and the 'C', consistency. Thus, as an acronym, a change leadership pun, and a metaphor about how humans and other two-eyed species take in visual information; two eyes ('Is') see ('C'). Thus 2IsC™ was born.

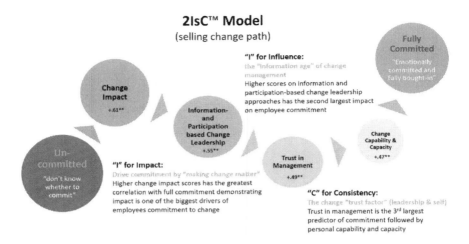

2IsC™ Model
(selling change path)

Change Impact +.61**

Un-committed "don't know whether to commit"

Information- and Participation- based Change Leadership +.55**

Trust in Management +.49**

Change Capability & Capacity +.47**

Fully Committed "Emotionally committed and fully bought-in"

"I" for Influence: the "information age" of change management
Higher scores on information and participation-based change leadership approaches has the second largest impact on employee commitment

"I" for Impact: Drive commitment by "making change matter"
Higher change impact scores has the greatest correlation with full commitment demonstrating impact is one of the biggest drivers of employees commitment to change

"C" for Consistency: The change "trust factor" (leadership & self)
Trust in management is the 3rd largest predictor of commitment followed by personal capability and capacity

Figure 4. Selling Change Path

The first **"I" for impact** refers to the fact that the significance or importance of the change was the highest contributing factor to highly engaged commitment. Higher change impact scores are the greatest predictor of highly engaged change commitment. Leaders who effectively demonstrate the impact and significance of planned or in-progress workplace changes have the highest chance of boosting their team member's commitment levels and achieving overall change success.

The second **"I" for influence** addresses how leaders communicate and approach change efforts in ways that drive commitment. Information-based leadership approaches fall under this category and information-based leadership was the second largest predictor of highly engaged change commitment.

Finally, the **"C" for consistency** refers to workers having a high degree of trust in both management and confidence in their own personal capacity and capability to perform effectively in the new environment. Trust in management as a predictive factor in the change commitment journey indicates the value of team members feeling that leaders will be consistent, straightforward, and will follow-through on commitments. Capability and capacity refers to the degree of confidence one has in their own abilities.

Based on the model, below are some key questions team members who hear about a major change at work will ask themselves (and each other) about the planned change or transformation.

Figure 6 summarizes each of the research-based factors that predict highly engaged commitment to change including change impact, information-based change leadership, participation-based change leadership, trust in management, and change capability and capacity.

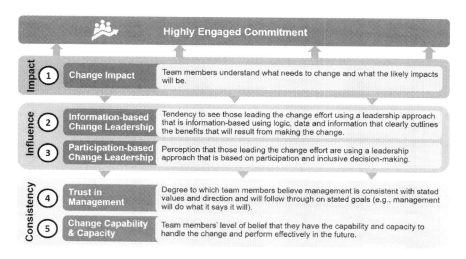

Figure 5. Highly engaged commitment model

For organizational leaders planning for and executing change initiatives, there are several questions linked to each of the five factors outlined below. These questions highlight the "answers" change leaders need to have in order to communicate changes in ways that bolster commitment. Questions include:

- **Impact focus:** If I work harder or differently, will I be able to change the proposed outcomes of the change. If yes, then commitment and motivation will increase.
- **Influence focus (information-based change leadership):** Do I have the information I need to make a serious mental and emotional commitment to support the proposed change?
- **Influence focus (participation-based change leadership):** Do I have a say in creating what the future of this organization will look like?
- **Consistency focus (trust in management):** Do I trust that my manager and the management team will look out for me and my department if I commit to the change they are proposing?
- **Consistency focus (personal capability and capacity):** Will I be successful if I adopt the new way of doing things?

In chapter 6, we will examine three different leaders who have led successful turnarounds at their organizations. In each case, a clear majority of their team members would have answered yes to each of these questions or, if not, those team members voluntarily opted to leave the organization. That is indicative of how critical each of these factors are to highly engaged change commitment. So how do we know that change commitment is linked to change outcomes? The change research bears this out. In chapter 1 we explored change management research showing 72% of change initiatives fail due to people related-issues. Impact-related change failures occurs when most team members do not think the change is worth committing themselves to. This comprises 39% of people-related change failures. Influence and Consistency change failures occur when leaders do not lead changes in ways that increase workers' motivation to commit to change. This comprises 33% of people-related change failures. So, from a purely numbers perspective, focusing on roughly 70% of the causes of change failures will increase the odds of change success by at least 2 times.

We have explored research that empirically shows how the importance of impact of proposed changes, change leadership strategy, and trust come together to drive highly engaged change commitment. These work in combination to create an environment of highly engaged change commitment. The research findings are summarized below:

1. High levels of change impact is the biggest predictor of highly engaged commitment to change
    - High-impact changes drive commitment irrespective of whether team members consider the change to be beneficial or harmful to themselves personally, their department, or the organization overall

2. Information-based change leadership strategies are the second biggest predictor of commitment to change
    - Leaders who adopt an information-based change leadership approach provide team members with a greater sense of justification for and legitimacy of the change initiative

3. Participation-based change leadership is the third-largest predictor of highly engaged change commitment
    - Leaders who are inclusive and provide opportunities for team members have a say in key decisions and helping to create future organizational changes will have teams with greater levels of "want to" change commitment

4. Higher levels of trust in management represented the fourth largest predictor of highly-engaged change commitment
    - Leaders who can garner the trust of their team members will have team members who are more committed to change in the organization

5. Higher levels of change commitment and capacity represents the fifth predictor of highly engaged change commitment

- Team members who believe they are capable of achieving and being successful during and after the change will have higher levels of change commitment.

So what can be done to get buy-in to planned changes at work? The key is to frame change-related messages in ways that will make people more inclined to commit to change at the beginning of and throughout the change process. The more the change message aligns to the mental processes the brain follows when making decisions, the more effective those messages will be. These can be thought of as influence factors. The next chapter outlines influence factors and practical ways to frame change initiatives in ways that will create and ignite commitment.

Making of a Commitment Model

There are a range of new and useful change management models for leaders and change management experts to choose from. Some are focused on whom and how often to communicate change while others are more leadership or agile/lean focused. The Impact, Influence, and Consistency model (2IsC™) is different in its focus on how to create highly engaged change commitment across a critical mass of change stakeholders.

Rather than simply going through the stages of a change management process, the 2IsC™ model assumes that people will be more engaged throughout each stage of the change and transformation process once they are committed to the overall purpose, goals and direction of the change. When the change management process is designed around assessing and creating commitment, the likelihood of delivering change successfully increases dramatically. How do we know this? We know change management processes that are grounded in traditional change models often fail because their core assumptions are flawed (see Faulty Change Assumptions). If we shift change models up to a strategy and outcome focus (and away from a tactical change plan focus) there are a series of outcomes change leaders should aim to deliver. By engaging with team members in these ways, change leaders enable attitude and behavioral changes that drive buy-in and commitment, and ultimately, successful change outcomes.

Rank	Highly Engaged Commitment Factor	Change Commitment Driver*
1	Change Impact	.61
2	Information-based Change Leadership	.58
3	Participation-based Change Leadership	.51
4	Trust in Management	.49
5	Change Capability & Capacity	.47
6	Job Satisfaction (engagement proxy)	.41
		*r-squared @ 0.01 significance level

Figure 6. Highly engaged commitment factors

In my research, I found six factors that were predictive of highly engaged change commitment including: Change Impact, Information-based Change Leadership, Participation-based Change Leadership, Trust in Management, Change Capability and Capacity, and Job Satisfaction. Together, each of these factors correlated with highly engaged change commitment ("want to" change).[36] To give you an intuitive sense of how to read the correlations, consider the fact that the correlation between smoking and cancer is 0.3. Each of the correlations between the highly engaged change commitment and the six factors I studied across 650 workers in retail and manufacturing sectors were between 0.4 and 0.6. These correlations suggest these factors are important enough to change behavior and can serve as a basis for leadership decisions.

The Impact Factor

The change impact factor refers to the fact that for team members to commit to change, they must first believe the change is important and has significance. Impact showed the highest correlation with highly engaged commitment. Impact represents the table stakes of change commitment because without it, even the most effective change leaders will be unable to generate enough momentum to get their teams moving.

Change focus (change impact)

We previously explored research showing that most team members tend to agree with proposed changes in principle at least. Most team members tend to agree with the need for transformation and proposed changes. This is further supported by employee engagement research showing that workers tend to be more engaged when the place they work is considered to be high performing. So the first challenge to overcome when building commitment is simply making the change seem important enough for people to care about it. Depending on the type of change this may be easier or more challenging. Some workplace changes such as a new organizational strategy, a culture change, or a merger may be inherently impactful enough that the urgency needed to engage large parts of the organization around them is easier. However, less transformative changes such as a new technology platform or new product development may touch only parts of the organization or may not be considered big enough for a critical mass of team members to rally around. In those cases, more work is needed upfront to make the case for "Why Change".

One of the most fascinating studies on this topic was research that examined results from three different studies encompassing 92 different change initiatives in different organizations representing twenty-one different industries including banking, engineering, health care, manufacturing, technology services, and utilities.[37] The researchers found that workers were less committed to changes that had a lower job impact even when those changes had favorable outcomes. That was mildly interesting. After all, even if you anticipate a positive outcome for a change at work but the impact of that change on you and your job is low, the average person probably will not care as much, hence, the lower levels of commitment. However, what was remarkable was the finding that employees' levels of commitment to change were greater for unfavorable, high-impact job changes with significant work unit impacts than they were for low-impact job changes. In other words, even when a change at work was expected to have an unfavorable outcome, the mere fact that it was perceived to have a higher impact on workers' jobs and their work unit was enough for them to show higher levels of change commitment.

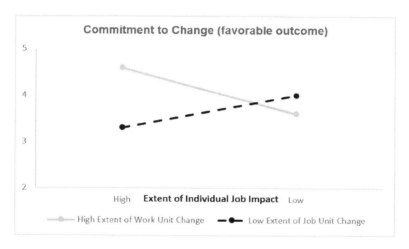

Figure 7. Commitment to Change Expected (favorable outcome)

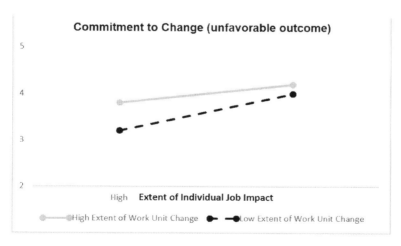

Figure 8. Commitment to Change (unfavorable outcome)

This cross-organization, cross-industry change research mirrored my research findings in which organizational changes with high job loss risk still achieved high levels of commitment when change impacts were high. Changes with clear, significant job impacts are associated with higher levels of worker commitment to change. We will explore options for increasing commitment in chapter 5 (Influence Factor #1 "Why Change").

Using Emotions to Convey Impact

Emotions are the lenses through which people assess information. Cognitive researchers have observed that the brain uses emotions as the grid through which it filters information it receives. The collection of emotions a person experiences at a given time is known as their emotional state and it influences how the brain processes choices. Studies show that positive emotions can boost comprehension, decision-making ability, and receptiveness to persuasive requests.[38,39] Conversely, when people are in a negative emotional state, their perceptions of people and events become more cynical. One study done at a medical technology firm found that workers' emotional states during an organizational crisis directly accounted for several key factors including perceived supervisory support, levels of cynicism, and psychological resilience.[40] In a different study comparing the effects of employee attitudes on customer service quality, researchers examined both the workers' attitudes and customers' ratings of service quality. Unsurprisingly, workers with more cynical attitudes exhibited more negative reactions towards their customers (e.g., expressed tension, were unfriendly) and the more negative reactions these employees showed towards their customers, the less satisfied customers were with the service quality.[41]

To fully grasp the impact emotional states have on decision-making, a group of researchers looked at how emotions affected decision-making in an area where no one, including the decision-makers themselves, believed emotions would have an influence—judicial rulings. In a study published in the *Proceedings of the National Academy of Sciences*, researchers found that when judges were in a positive emotional state, they granted parole 65 percent of the time.[42] Seems reasonable, but when the same judges were in a negative emotional state (e.g., tired, hungry, or just ready to go home at the end of the day), the probability of the judges granting parole was nearly zero. Few judges who have trained for years and practiced law for decades would admit or even see their own decision-making process as a function of their emotional states but the evidence, in this case, proves otherwise.

Undoubtedly, emotions play an outsized role in organizational processes and should not be ignored or dismissed when crafting a change-focused selling approach to organizational change. Even after "the facts" of a proposed organizational change have been made clear, change leaders must connect with the emotions that will compel team members to want to commit to the change. Emotion-based impact is best conveyed through the use of relevant story-telling that has the following three characteristics:

1. Are easily remembered after "the facts" are forgotten
2. Provide a sense of authenticity
3. Are more easily relatable on a personal level

We will explore additional emotion-focused approaches that support highly engaged change commitment when we examine the Influence factors.

Influence Factors

There were two key influence factors that correlate with highly engaged commitment to change. These included worker perceptions of leaders who led change efforts using an information-based change leadership strategy followed closely by participation-based change leadership. Team members who perceive an information-based change leadership approach tend to see those leading the change effort adopting a communication approach that motivates team members to commit to change using logic, data, and information that clearly outlines the benefits that will result from making the change. It is easy to see how this approach operates synergistically with higher levels of change impact since change leaders who are high on information-based change leadership are more likely to better articulate the impact the change will have and outline the benefits and value it can produce.

Participation-based change leaders are perceived to lead change efforts with a focus on inclusive decision making

---

Crowdsourcing Change Commitment

When it comes to change, getting alignment between frontline managers and executives is no small feat. The C-suite and executive focus is often future-focused while front-line managers are frequently preoccupied with the day-to-day operational realities. In an effort to align these two perspectives, one transportation company implemented a crowdsourcing platform where upper management could share business news and concerns keeping them up at night, and frontline managers could weigh in with their own views.

Customer-facing managers posted questions on the platform that C-level executives addressed at all-hands meetings. In a matter of weeks, nearly 70% of frontline managers shared ideas for the company's B2C strategy using the crowdsourcing mechanisms and open communications. The overwhelming support convinced the company's chief executive that changing the sales model was the right move, and rank-and-file managers agreed. Not only did this approach work as an Influence and Consistency-focused tool, it also enabled team members to feel more engaged because frontline managers felt heard and management took their opinions into account.

---

and design. The approach motivates team members to change by listening to and gathering input from those impacted by and involved in the change. In participation-based change, leaders may get stakeholder input through a combination of direct participation or by having stakeholders provide input on key design elements or decisions.

Influence focus (Information-based Change Leadership)

So which comes first, thinking or behavior? The research is not 100% clear on this with some studies showing that behavior follows mental evaluations of the pros and cons and others showing that cognition follows behavior. While it is beyond the scope of this book to solve which comes first, my personal opinion is that for more complex, higher-order behaviors that require evaluation and judgement (a major organizational change that will require learning and performing new sets of behaviors and tasks for instance), cognition comes first and behavior follows. On the whole, people will evaluate the factors associated with changing their behavior then make a decision about whether it is worth it to make those changes. An apt analogy is the difference between making a purchase decision about what to drink versus what car to buy. Because the impact of making a decision about what to drink is so low, the average person will put comparatively less mental energy into making that decision versus a decision about what car to purchase. That difference is the reason I suspect my research uncovered the fact that information-based change strategies showed a slightly higher link to highly engaged change commitment. Because team members first evaluated what impact the change would have for them personally and then made a determination about whether or not it was worth it, the process of learning about the change and understanding its possible impacts helped better facilitate the decision-making process required to commit to the change. This finding is consistent with meta-analytic research showing that simply thinking about behavior increases the likelihood that a person will act upon that behavior.[43]

Influence focus (Participation-based Change Leadership)

After impact and information-based change leadership, the next most predictive factor of employee commitment is participative change leadership. In classic change management literature and research, the participation-based approach is considered the gold-standard of change commitment. Participation-based change leadership refers to the idea that individuals will be more committed to organizational change when they are involved in multiple aspects of the decision-making, design, development, and implementation of organizational changes.[44,45] Participation-based approaches to change as a motivator of workers' buy-in and commitment traces its roots back to some of the earliest research on organizational change in the 1940s. More recent research has shown that when employees participate in the decision-making process, they may have a better understanding of and perceptions of the change (increased value), show higher levels of engagement with colleagues and managers about the change (improved relationships), and report enhanced job satisfaction and performance.[46]

Team members want to feel engaged and empowered at work. Given the extensive literature around benefits of participation-based change leadership and the generally-accepted notion that higher levels of worker involvement improves organizational change, the intent is not to delve into the importance or value of involving employees in the change process. Instead, the question of participation-based changes become more important in change contexts where the speed is paramount and the ability for individuals from multiple levels of the organization to have a say in the change process is limited or not feasible. In an ideal world, change leaders would have sufficient time to clearly articulate the rationale for change and provide opportunities to gain input from workers at multiple levels, across multiple departments in the change roll-out as they progress through each stage of the Change Curve (awareness, understanding, adoption, and commitment).[47] However, as the rate of change continues to increase, organizational leaders increasingly gloss over or simply ignore the power of more participatory approaches.

Consistency Factors

Consistency, at its core, is nothing more than the glue that holds impact and influence together. The core of consistency is trust. For change to move fluidly, team members need to have an adequate to moderate to high level of trust that organizational leaders will do what they say they will and that leaders are themselves committed to the change process. If the organization's leaders don't support the change truthfully and visibly, it will be hard to bring people

> **"...you have to get people in your organization to see the need for change as existential...you have to be all in—you must make bold, sustained commitment to the change."**
>
> - Jeff Immelt, former CEO, GE

onboard. After the project kicks off and after the initial set of high-energy meetings, the proverbial excitement of the project will naturally begin to wane. During this 'middle phase' of the project or change effort, momentum and energy for the change are at their lowest levels. The initial energy for what prompted the change effort in the first place is gone and the end is not yet close enough for team members to feel as though the end is in sight. The consistency factor serves as the gravitational force that will sustain movement towards a new way of doing things. Without consistency, priorities will begin to shift and interest in the transformation effort will subside. Quick tips for maintaining consistency throughout the change process include:

1. Having key leaders and influencers make public commitments to the change effort.
2. Making heroes out of those who support the change effort through rewards and public recognition.
3. Demonstrating early success through pilot programs and engaging status updates.

The Trust Factor

The first ingredient of consistency is trust. At its core, trust refers to the willingness of one person or a group to be vulnerable to another even when there is a risk of harm. Trust in management is really a measure of how willing team members are to rely on top managers' judgement in situations that may be risky or potentially harmful. My research showed that higher levels of managerial trust and personal levels of change capability were associated with highly engaged commitment to change. These are mutually reinforcing constructs. When team members believe change leaders are supportive of the change initiative it prompts team members to put personal effort towards the change initiative. Research shows that as team members are given opportunities to practice new behaviors and gain associated skills, their commitment to change also increases. Providing opportunities for hands-on learning and leaders who role model future behaviors reinforce key change-focused messages and allow time to develop the skills required to succeed in the future. A consistency-focused approach to leading change will provide team members with time to practice and acquire the skills necessary to perform proficiently in the future state.

One of the leading researchers on interpersonal and organizational trust, Paul Zak, found a clear relationship between trust and organizations' financial performance. Employees in high-trust organizations have 50% higher levels of productivity, are 76% more engaged, and have 106% more energy at work.[48] In short, trust serves as the cultural lubricant that makes cross-team and employee-manager interactions more seamless and effective. For organizations looking to improve the effectiveness of their transformation efforts, one way to do that is to foster a high-trust environment. Trust is built when there is consistency of behavior and practice. Trust in management develops over time when team members know what they can expect from their management team and, in this way, trust is a measure of management consistency. How consistently do managers and executives words match their actions? Today's workers prefer communications and interactions that are transparent, genuine, and personalized and want to feel their voices are being heard.

> **"It's every interaction that makes or breaks your trust."**
>
> - Renee Wynn, CIO, NASA

Transformational Leadership, Leadership that Creates Buy-In

Leadership is a key ingredient in the consistency aspect of the 2IsC™ model. In the past, leaders would give orders and team members were simply expected to do as they were told. Increasingly, that autocratic leadership is losing its cache and effectiveness. Indeed, in my research, power-based leadership was highly negatively correlated with engaged commitment to change. Today's organizational transformations require leaders who are themselves transformative. These leaders guide their teams by encouraging and enabling them--creating an atmosphere that energizes team members and fosters excitement about future possibilities. This is supported by neuroscience research that shows that decision making, problem solving, and collaboration all increase in more supportive, low-threat environments.[49]

Organizational management researchers have identified transformational leaders as individuals who are able to effectively appeal to followers' sense of values and are able to get them to see a higher vision and encourage them to exert effort toward achieving that vision.[50] In line with more distributed, self-organizing models of today's organizations, transformational leaders are characterized by their ability to create and communicate a vision and foster opportunities that allow followers to bring their best to work.[51] The ability to establish personal credibility that causes followers to trust, admire, and identify with the leader's goals are also traits of transformational leaders. Additionally, researchers have found that transformational leaders excite their followers and team intellectually and show care for their needs.[52] What becomes clear when thinking about transformational leaders in the context of transformational organizational change is the fact that this leadership style aligns extremely well with multiple aspects of highly engaged change commitment including information-based change leadership (intellectual excitement), participation-based change leadership, change impact (creating a vision), and establishing trust. Indeed, research shows that transformational leadership is positively linked to change commitment irrespective of whether change leadership is considered effective or not.[53] In other words, whether or not effective change management practices are in place, transformational leaders are able to generate commitment to change among their teams.

The Turnover Issue

Employee turnover during periods of change is an indirect measure of workforce levels of trust in the management team. Turnover during periods of significant organizational change is not only indicative of whether or not team members agree with the overall direction of the change but is also a measure of trust—a factor that often receives less attention in discussions about change-driven turnover. There is a tendency to dismiss employees who leave as simply unwilling to get onboard or unable to accept transformation decisions and the associated outcomes. Seen in a different light, turnover during organizational change represents a lack of trust. If team members do not believe organizational leaders are themselves consistently committed to change efforts and do not think those same leaders will support them in the new ways of doing things, then trust in leadership and the proposed changes will start to decline along with commitment to change.

Keeping Things Moving

The final aspect of the consistency factor involves the ways in which change leaders can keep the momentum for change going long after the initial hype and excitement of the change wears off. As former GE, Jeff Immelt put it, "transformation takes grit and requires staying power." The middle and end of transformational changes can be some of the most dangerous times in the transformation lifecycle because other priorities and newer changes can begin to divert critical resources, time, and attention away from the change or transformation effort. Particularly for longer-term change and transformation projects that can span months or years, team members become tired or simply 'ready for it to be over'. Or, turnover leaves gaps in the people and commitment 'infrastructure' needed to bring the transformation initiative over the finish line where it becomes ingrained in the daily work life, behaviors, thinking and culture of the transformed organization. The solution is three consistency principles:

1. Pace change and transformation
2. Create minimum sufficient wins
3. Include the team

Pacing change and transformation refers to the ability to avoid the temptation to introduce too many changes at once. Instead, effective change organizations introduce a focused set of prioritized organizational changes that can be effectively introduced, managed, and tracked with clear milestones, and brought to completion before the next major change is introduced. In the event the landscape shifts and a change initiative that has been introduced is no longer needed, change leaders should clearly articulate that shift and introduce the new direction and set of priorities and how they are different than the previous change. Executives whose middle managers complain that "we've tried things like this before and failed" receive reinforcement when yet another change initiative fails. By creating a clear line of differentiation between old and new change initiatives, change leaders can mitigate the risk of change fatigue in which team members disengage with current and future change initiatives because they feel either overwhelmed by too many different change initiatives or become cynical and resistant toward future changes because they never saw any of them become successful.

Creating minimum sufficient wins means that for change initiatives to maintain their momentum, clear, tangible results need to be achieved and made visible. This can come in the form of status meeting updates, a change tracking system, a company newsletter or any combination of the above, but the consistency-focused lifeblood of high-engaged commitment is the ability to demonstrate that change efforts are producing results. Change initiatives should be crafted around those decisions and actions that will have the biggest, quickest impact. Without rigorous prioritization, the organization will fall victim to change overload in which every change is deemed important and therefore none are actually. Change leaders and executives need to make difficult decisions about what change is most important and how they need to be resourced and in what order to ensure change success. Hosting change and transformation meetings in which real topics such as resource allocation, required decision-making across multiple functions, and what's needed to accelerate operations and implementation are the real topics of consistency-focused change. Of course, conversations such as these can only be facilitated by a culture of trust and transparency (see The Trust Factor).

Include the team means that change leaders need to incorporate inputs and suggestions from team members throughout the change process (not just at the beginning). At the beginning of the change process, it's somewhat intuitive to include members of the team but as the change progresses, more attention and consideration needs to be paid to ensure team members remain connected to the change process. At one global energy company, executives set a goal of becoming more engaged, involved, and more effective communicators with their teams. So, did they implement an elaborate, multi-million dollar change program? No at all. To maintain engagement and commitment consistency, the leaders created a WhatsApp group message thread for weekly check-ins to share their accomplishments. Nearly half the group only needed a text reminder to complete the weekly check-in, and the rest followed after seeing messages from colleagues who had already completed their tasks.[54]

In the 2IsC™ model, the consistency factor brings together all the elements of effective impact and influence factors with extraordinary results.

Barriers to Highly Engaged Change

The research behind the 2IsC™ model also uncovered the flip side of highly engaged commitment to change including several factors that reduced commitment, including power-based change leadership, job insecurity, and employment dependence. The key is to identify when these approaches are being used unintentionally (or intentionally) and take steps to reduce this perception. Chapter 6 contains success stories of leaders who were (and still are) leveraging effective change leadership approaches to drive significant turnaround efforts despite significant organizational and financial headwinds.

As I was conducting research on factors that bolstered highly engaged change commitment, I also uncovered several factors that seemed to have more deleterious impacts on engaged commitment. These included power-based change leadership, job insecurity, and employment dependence. The reality is that transformation efforts often exacerbate attitudes, issues, and pressures that already exist in the workplace. Transformational change efforts can produce pressure cooker environments where poor leadership behaviors are accelerated yet more positive elements of workers' attitudes can be put on display.

Barrier #1: Power-based change leadership

Power-based change leadership refers to the perception that those leading the change are using power and their positions of authority to get team members to comply with the change. Often, power-based change leaders exert themselves in the form of extremely ambitious people who tend to steamroll their colleagues, destroy teamwork, and put their own agendas ahead of the organization's interests. Leaders who take this approach either knowingly or inadvertently motivate team members to change using threats or forced compliance. In power-based change, leaders may get stakeholders to commit to changes by directly or indirectly threatening to take something away. Through their actions, these leaders make it clear that without compliance, some unwanted event will happen such as the loss of a job, lack of promotion, or not receiving a pay increase. Perceived use of power-based change leadership had the highest negative correlation with highly engaged commitment and therefore represents the biggest threat to commitment for leaders who want to generate buy-in for change initiatives. Few people want to feel as though they are being forced to accept organizational changes or that leaders are using threats and coercion to lead change, yet this is exactly how power-based change leaders are perceived and it was the biggest factor associated with reduced levels of highly engaged change commitment. I suspect most leaders do not intend to use this approach when leading change initiatives but may inadvertently adopt this approach in a rush towards results.

Barrier # 2: Job Insecurity

Job insecurity came out as the second largest barrier to highly engaged change commitment. The research on job insecurity shows that it is both an uncertainty factor (not knowing if you will remain employed) as well as a significant source of stress. People who are concerned about their job security are less satisfied with their jobs, are less involved in their work, less committed to their organization, have poorer performance, and are more likely to behave in ways that will negatively impact the organization such as calling in sick and coming in late.[55,56] Given all the negative outcomes associated with job insecurity, it is no small wonder why it is the second highest threat to highly engaged change commitment. During times of organizational change and transformation, concerns about job security come into greater focus as team members may begin to wonder if the changes will result in job losses or changes to their jobs that will make their work more difficult.

Barrier # 3: Job Dependence

A bit unexpectedly, employment or job dependence was the third factor that was negatively correlated with highly engaged commitment to change. Employment dependence refers to the inability to easily find employment at a different organization and the extent to which a person is financially dependent on their current employer. My research found that higher rates of employment/job dependence were associated with decreased levels of commitment. I believe the reason for this rests in the idea that people undergoing transformational change at the workplace perceive job dependence in much the same way they perceive power-based change leadership. It causes them to feel forced to change rather than an active participant who would get to evaluate the change process on its merits (information-based change) or as someone who can provide input (e.g., participation-based change).

While power-based change leadership, job insecurity, and job dependence were the factors that were shown to reduce highly engaged commitment to change, in the next section, we will explore factors that lead to outright resistance to change. For change leaders looking to maximize their impact and influence, they will want to ensure they are addressing both sides of the change equation by increasing commitment and reducing resistance.

Emotional, Mental, and Behavioral Resistance to Change

I was recently consulting the CEO of a multinational healthcare technology firm. The company was well positioned for future growth and had already begun making strides in growing its customer base but with the newfound success came concerns about its ability to provide the same level of exceptional service to its long-time existing major clients which had become accustomed to receiving dedicated, "white glove" treatment. As the company began to shift its focus to growing new business, its five largest long-time, revenue-generating clients began noticing quality issues that were starting to impact the company's brand perception. In an effort to maintain its existing clients and continue to grow, the CEO initiated a change effort to temporarily shift staff and resources away from new business clients in order to address quality and system issues that were important to the existing clients. Seems fairly reasonable, right? But what the CEO had not anticipated was the amount of internal resistance he would encounter by attempting to shift, even temporarily, the company's focus.

Change Resistance in Context

All organizational change initiatives exist in a particular context and that context sets the tone for how change will be led. The particular context of this firm was that of an organization poised for growth and new business with an operating model that was uniquely structured to support those aims. The company's team members were all ready to move forward and all systems were go. That was until the CEO pulled the proverbial rug from everyone's feet by essentially proposing a change in strategy that would move the company in a direction that was completely opposite of the one they had been primed to follow. As the "surge" to improve quality commenced, signs of resistance started to emerge ranging from slow work on existing client issues to cross-team complaints about having to shift focus and grumbling. While no one said it outright, the resistance message was clear—team members felt this new approach violated what they expected and what they had been told and they were not happy.

> **Why Dealing with Resistance Matters**
>
> A recent study compared what happens with resistance to organizational change over time. In examining 40 healthcare clinics undergoing a 3-year period of significant organizational changes, workers' resistance to change attitudes became stronger (rather than weaker) over time. The results suggest that workers' resistance attitudes become more entrenched over time leading to lower levels of organizational commitment and lower levels of perceived organizational effectiveness.

Resistance to change has a long, storied history in the change management literature with a number of perspectives akin to the classic nature vs nurture debate in psychology. From a more nature-focused definition of resistance to change, resistance is viewed as a natural (expected) reaction anytime a new way of doing things is introduced. More nurture-oriented definitions of resistance define it as being more a symptom of ineffective leadership and communication. The reality is that both are true. We have all met people who, no matter what the benefit or value of changing is, will have some (or a lot) of objections to it. On the other hand, there are times when change is introduced but due to poor communication, misaligned expectations, negative history, or the inability to effectively 'sell the change', otherwise rational and open-minded people will become resistant to new ways of doing things. Just like in the example of the financial institution highlighted in chapter 2, simply by modifying their 'change story' from an executive/managerial focus to one that's more societal, purposeful, and customer-focused, the company saw an increase in change motivation scores of 61%. Because both nature and nurture resistance factors are present in the change process, I included measures of both in my research to identify the drivers of effective change leadership. Specifically, I measured three types of change resistance including emotional resistance ("This change makes me feel uncomfortable"), mental resistance ("I don't agree with the direction this change is taking us"), and behavioral resistance (e.g., "I have or plan to behave in ways that show my resistance"). Each of these resistance types were highly correlated with each other (all above r-squared of .78) suggesting that when one type is present, the other types will be present themselves as well. For instance, a person who is emotionally resistant will also think the change is a bad idea (mental resistance) and is more likely speak badly about the change to others (behavioral resistance). Much like a negative political ad campaign ad gone viral, resistance to change can create a negative feedback loop in which people who are on the fence or only mildly in favor of the change effort begin receiving alternative messages from change "resisters" that begin to erode their confidence in the value of the change effort.

The Resistance Findings

Figure 9 outlines the factors that reduce the three resistance types meaning that when change leaders increase these factors, resistance to change can be reduced. We see several parallels between the three resistance types and highly engaged change commitment. The first being that change impact was the biggest factor in reducing both emotional and behavioral resistance to change. While easier said than done, by increasing investments in impact-focused communications (e.g., outlining the value/benefit of changing, why this change matters), change leaders get a double benefit of improved change commitment and reduced change resistance. Said another way, the greater team members' perception of the impact of the change, the more committed, and less resistant, they will be to change.

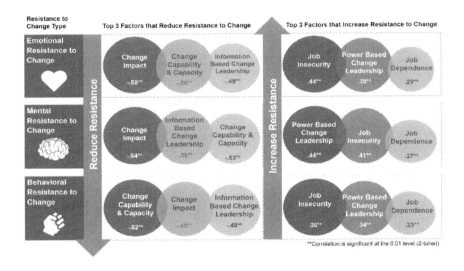

Figure 9. Top 3 factors that increase and reduce commitment to change

Job insecurity and power-based change leadership were among the top three factors associated with increased levels of all three resistance to change types. When introducing and leading organizational change, leaders should be mindful of communications and behaviors that make team members feel their jobs are threatened and reduce perceptions that organizational changes are being led in ways that make team members feel they must change "or else". Increasing trust in management and perceptions of information-based change leadership were among the top factors shown to reduce job insecurity. For power-based change leadership, increasing perceptions of information-based change leadership was shown to reduce perceptions of power-based change leadership. In short, by following the 2IsC™ model, change leaders can increase highly engaged commitment to change and reduce team member resistance.

Bringing it all together

In change contexts, leaders who "sell" change to their team members through a combination of telling an informed, compelling story about current and future impacts and then role-modelling those behaviors will have an advantage in terms of getting their team to commit to those changes. An effective 2IsC™ approach to selling change addresses Impact, Influence, and Consistency by crafting communications that answer the following questions:

Impact	Influence	Consistency
"This is what's possible"	"This is why we're doing this"	"Here's how leadership will support you"
"Here's what's at stake"	"Here's who will benefit and why"	"Here's what you need to be successful along the way"
	"Here's how you can be part of this"	

Organizational change and transformation will continue to be managed by people, many of whom will need to do so on a more frequent basis and across multiple organizational levels. To create highly-engaged change commitment or "sell change" most effectively, change leaders should clearly demonstrate the impact of the change by outlining the value, meaning, and benefits of the change. These leaders will also need to influence change using information and participation-based change leadership approaches. Creating consistency in the form of trust-building and building capability and capacity are what's needed to create a full, end-to-end approach for selling change in any organization.

While perfecting their organizational change approach based on the 2IsC™ model, transformational leaders will want to watch out for barriers to highly engaged change commitment including emotional, mental, and behavioral resistance to change. These barriers include power-based change leadership, job insecurity, and job dependence. By leveraging these research-based insights, change leaders will have a cadre of change-specific leadership tools that will improve change leadership organization-wide and therefore the ability to effectively transform their organizations. When change is sold using a combination of Impact, Influence, and Consistency, organizational change and transformations can be delivered successfully and consistently.

Chapter 4 - Using Impact and Influence to Sell Change

"If your actions inspire others to dream more, learn more, do more, and become more, you are a leader."

John Quincy Adams, 6th President of the United States of America

Sitting in the 10th floor conference room overlooking a multi-screen power grid monitor of the United States, the view was straight out of a science fiction thriller. As I sat, surrounded by a team of senior HR and IT executives and various project managers, I felt like this was the team that would make it happen for one of the world's largest producers of wind energy. There was enough clout and expertise on the team to bring to bear the people and budgetary resources needed to overhaul the performance management process across all organizational levels. The project team had the buy-in and backing from the CEO--himself a career-long employee at this prestigious energy firm having risen through the ranks after starting as a linesman installing and repairing power lines. As the external change management lead and project co-lead, I managed our small yet very capable team over the course of the next 9 months in all things related to changing the company's performance management systems and processes. We adopted an iterative agile methodology and introduced the approach to project leaders with a long history steeped in Waterfall. We created a 3-year roadmap that aligned to technical as well as practical best practices. We mapped our future-state process flows and brought onboard an SAP technical expert to ensure all the backend data and systems were accurately integrated. We wanted to ensure that one of the first implementations of this type was a resounding success.

Approximately two months into the project the first signs of trouble began to emerge. During our weekly meetings, I began noticing that key design decisions were repeatedly delayed. This is not unusual, particularly during a project of this size and scope, but after the third week of delays and several escalation attempts I knew a different approach was needed to ensure the project stayed on track. After careful consideration and multiple discussions among the project team, I realized the core problem--the executives who needed to make the key decisions did not fully understand the impact their decisions would have. As a result, they were reluctant to make decisions that would put their functions, the organization, or their careers at risk. We were in fact speaking different languages. The project team was speaking the language of Human Resources and IT which carried very little meaning for the heads of Legal, Risk, and Supply Chain. After coming to this realization, I spent several hours one evening in my hotel lobby creating decision-making templates that clearly outlined each "open" decision we were waiting on. The templates outlined the 3-5 impacts each decision would have for the various functional areas (HR, talent, legal, IT) as well as the business impacts associated with selecting option A vs option B. I then asked the system and process experts on my project team to review and fill-in 'open areas' on the impact chart for accuracy and validity. Figure 10 contains the template I created that night.

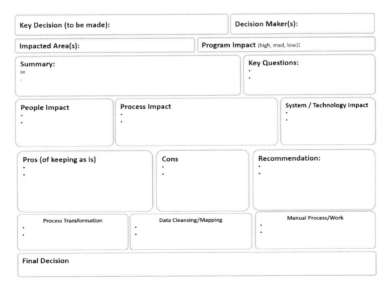

Figure 10. Change decision-making template

Although it still took several more weeks to hammer out the details and make sure the right stakeholders were made aware of and able to opine on key decisions, the episode highlighted a key aspect of the overall 2IsC™ model, which is that impact and influence are constantly interacting throughout the change process. Executives with the influence needed to make the change-related decisions were well aware of, and indeed committed to, the need to overhaul the company's performance process in order to recruit and move talent around the organization in meaningful ways that would support the long term health and sustainability of this future-focused energy company. However, without a complete understanding of how the change would impact their particular areas of responsibility, the change process ground to a halt. This, coupled with the fact that this organization made decisions in a consensus-driven manner meant that the transformation process could have easily died on the vine. How? We know from the change management research that most change initiatives fail. Project delays and cost overruns are often cited as the reasons why, but where do those come from? More often than not, it's due to people and leadership disconnects. The makings of this were at play at the energy client. Left to their devices, the executives who were consulted (but not owners or sponsors) would have delayed key decisions until the project hit a critical point of no return or a miracle last minute decision-making meeting was called. That is no

"…change leaders should focus their efforts on framing the change in ways that will increase commitment both when the change is introduced and throughout each stage of the change process"

way to effectively run an organization nor is it any way to run an effective organizational transformation. Since change commitment is rarely only about value or usefulness of the change itself (as we saw in chapter 2 most people are aligned to the goals of change initiatives), change leaders should focus their efforts on framing the change in ways that will increase commitment both when the change is introduced and throughout each stage of the change process.

Neuroscientists, psychologists, behavioral scientists, organizational researchers and behavioral economists have been hard at work uncovering the mental processes that affect decision-making and behavior. In the following sections, we will explore these findings in the context of organizational change to derive insights about what it really takes to influence stakeholders and sell change more effectively throughout the organization. Specially, there are four "selling change questions" you will want to answer to drive the highest levels of change commitment:

- Why Change?
- Why Now?
- Why You?
- Why Your Change?

Change Influence factor #1: Why Change?

The first and most effective way to influence organizational change is to help people understand why a change is needed in the first place. This is one of the most important parts of an effective change strategy because once the 'why' of change is fully appreciated and understood, it lays the groundwork for the other change influence factors.

The why change factor is based on the status quo bias which is the tendency people have to remain in their current position. 2017 Nobel Prize winner in economics, Richard Thaler, said in his book, *Misbehaving: The Making of Behavioral Economics,* "In physics, an object in a state of rest stays that way, unless something happens. People act the same way: they stick with what they have unless there is some good reason to switch". When you hear people say, "they are stuck in their ways" they are referring to the status quo bias. As humans, we are hardwired to associate greater levels of risk with something new and novel than with something we already have or are already comfortable with.[57] As a result, what leaders often perceive as "resistance" is really nothing more than the normal human tendency to not automatically leap into an unknown and potentially risky situation.

"It's because we're changing what your culture is used to, you have to educate them about the value. You have to essentially sell it a little bit…"

-Jason Jarrett, global head of Financial Systems and the Reporting Center of Excellence, Alere

Effective change leaders know they need to overcome this tendency by helping team members understand why a change will be worth the "risk" but too often, change leaders simply "tell" their team that a change is needed rather than clearly illustrating why the change is needed (information-based change leadership) or allowing them to discover the need for change on their own (participation-based change leadership). The best way to gain change commitment is to help team members fully understand the problems that make a change necessary. Until a critical number of team members realize there is a problem that needs to be addressed, it is unlikely enough momentum will be generated to make the change successful. In the following chapters, I refer to this as 'Impact'. John Kotter refers to this as creating a sense of urgency. The reality is that more organizational changes fail to be realized because team members resist change by maintaining the status quo. More often than not, it is simply easier for team members to continue operating as they always have unless there is a compelling reason to change. In chapter 6, we explore how Sharon Price, CEO of Build-A-Bear, created impact by directly addressing the 'Why' change influence factor. One approach to illustrating the need for change is the following 3-step approach:

- **Step 1:** Find problems by conveying challenging insights and asking questions
- **Step 2:** Identify the cause and scope of problems
- **Step 3:** Make problems hurt - Help your team understand the painful consequences of allowing the problem to continue

Find Problems: Problems are one of the biggest commitment factors because it is a primary motivating factor. Commitment factors refer to the set of conditions that cause team members to want to commit to change. Showing team members they have a problem that must be solved is not always the easiest task because often they are part of the process or system that is causing (or sustaining) the problem so they will not see a reason to make a change. On the positive side, once they are aware of the problem and have a desire to solve it, they will tend to view the change as necessary and become even more motivated to commit to changing.

One way to find problems is by challenging the status quo with key insights and questions that compel your team members to think about how things could be improved or asking team members to identify these. Once you have the list of problems, begin by linking proposed changes to that problem set to generate buy-in. Of course, truthfulness and transparency are paramount. Proposed changes that have little or no real relationship to problems or the root causes of those problems will have little or no value in bolstering commitment but when those two align, the net effect can be quite powerful. Examples of problem-linked questions include:

- What if your workload could be reduced by 20% in the next 6 months?
- How would you feel if we were able to payout bonuses next year?
- Our top 3 competitors are transitioning to an Agile methodology for product design, where will we be 3 years from now if we don't?
- What if I told you we could reinvest 10% of our revenues into helping 12% more constituents?

Identify the cause and scope of problems: Sometimes teams know they have a problem and have already begun raising issues. Tap into that already existing wellspring of energy. By identifying problems and asking the right questions to surface deeper issues, change leaders can earn the right to help solve the problem. This is where the power of listening can be leveraged. Often, new leaders will go on 'listening tours' when they transition to a new position to get perspective on common issues facing a cross-section of teams. When used effectively, these 'tours' have the benefit of helping leaders gain credibility and also better enables them to propose solutions designed to address the issues raised. If team members do not believe you can help solve some of the most significant concerns for themselves or the organization overall, they will be much less receptive to changing. Alternatively, if the changes you are proposing fail to adequately address problems and issues team members struggle with on a daily basis, they too will be less receptive to adopting those changes. When it comes to influencing change commitment, the ability to identify problems and their causes is a key differentiator.

Make problems hurt: Problems are not enough. To motivate change commitment, team members must see and feel the negative impact their problems are producing or could produce in the future. At an organizational level, this may be a loss of market share or clients. At the department level, that may mean a loss of key team members or missing performance targets. This is also the reason many purely visionary or utopian change initiatives fail to gain traction. For example, being an "industry leader" is not compelling enough to motivate, whereas the ability to make a profit that will translate into a bonus is (see chapter 6 'Transformation Case Study #3 - Building Buy-In at Build-A-Bear').

Cultivating your team's understanding of the cause and scope of their problems cannot be underestimated. The 'why change' influence factor is what the next set of influence factors are based on and represents the first stage of the neurologically-focused change commitment process that matches the way the brain makes commitment decisions.

Change Influence factor #2: Why Now?

Once the need for the change has been clearly established, the next step is to help team members understand why waiting to solve the problem is not an option. Many change initiatives fail due to a lack of urgency. Team members who would otherwise buy-in to the need for change and future vision often disengage if they sense change is not imminent or there is no real plan or course of action in the near-term.

A two-fold approach to creating a sense of urgency is presenting actions related to the change that team members can begin right away. In cases where a clear solution or approach to the future-state vision has not yet been fully established, start by having team members create a set of 'move forward' options. The added benefit of starting the commitment process with action is that you begin leveraging the power of cognitive dissonance.

How does this work? In an infamous laboratory psychology experiment, 71 participants were given an extremely boring task to complete (turning pegs in a peg board for 1 hour).[58] Afterwards, they were told to tell the next set of participants that the task was interesting and were paid either $1 or $20 to do so. When asked how they really felt about the task, participants who were paid $1 rated the obviously boring task as more fun and enjoyable than those who were paid $20. Why? The act of lying created dissonance or a gap between participants' thoughts or perceptions and the actual experience. For the $20 group, there was little dissonance because lying was easily justified due to the greater sum of money they received (they were adequately compensated) but the $1 group had a real problem--they completed a boring task for an hour and lied to someone about it. The only way to reduce this dissonance was by aligning their beliefs to their actions. The $1 dollar group did this by changing how they felt about completing the task. They began to believe the task was actually less boring than it was. By doing this they reduced their cognitive dissonance and felt better about the task and having lied about it.

The moral of this story is not about how to effectively engage others in unethical behavior, but instead, to highlight how commitment to even less-than-desirable changes can be influenced by assigning simple tasks to impacted team members (participation-based influence factor). The process of working on a change generates its own momentum because working towards change makes it increasingly difficult to disparage it or have negative beliefs about it. Doing something or anything related to the change has the effect of increasing commitment and reducing resistance.

As a change leader, one proven way to intentionally create commitment is by having team members do something to demonstrate the impact of the change. Because different organizational changes require different change approaches, the following 3 scenarios outline the best approach for the Why Now influence factor:

Scenario 1 - There are several ways to approach the change and any one of those options can be selected and approaches taken….

- *Suggested change approach:* assign team members actions to create options on ways to tackle the change.

Scenario 2 - If options for change are limited or non-existent...

- *Suggested change approach:* Present change options to team members and have them choose which approach they think represents the best way to move forward.

Scenario 3 - Leaders have already decided on a course of action...

- *Suggested change approach:* Ensure team members understand the future state vision and the actions required to achieve it then assign actions.

Change Influence factor #3: Why You?

Even if a change has been shown to be needed and even if a majority of organizational members believe something needs to change and even if they are, at a high-level, committed to changing, often, the best clarion calls for change go unheeded. Why? More often than it not it's the messenger. While there are a number of leadership factors that affect how successful a change will be, a key principle to keep in mind when leading change is summed up in media theorist Marshall McLuhan's phrase, "the medium is the message" by which he meant the source of the message influences how it is received. When change stakeholders and co-creators are first coming to understand that a particular change or new direction is needed, they are evaluating the messenger just as much, if not more, than the message about what needs to change. A well-designed, well-executed, and needed change is only as effective as the change leader or leadership team in place to guide the change initiative. One example is health insurer Aetna. In the early 2000s, following four different CEOs in five years and multiple attempts to change the culture, John W. Rowe, MD, came in and was able to begin effecting much-needed changes and was very successful at doing so.[59] How? Rowe was seen as a change leader who both understood the need for change as well as the cultural elements of Aetna's commitment to customers in a way that previous leaders had not. He was the embodiment of credibility as physician in a health service provider but in addition, he demonstrated an ability and willingness to understand and leverage Aetna's strong culture. This elevated him to the position of being viewed as having the credibility to take the organization to its needed next stage of growth. His leadership approach and who he was enabled him to increase commitment and reduce resistance where others had failed.

Approaches for improving the 'Why You?' influence factor include reducing risk by building trust. Trust and risk can be thought of as opposite ends of a spectrum. When trust is low, people are less willing to move forward. The fear response is triggered and individuals retreat into fight or flight mode (both forms of resistance to change). Naturally that is not an ideal place for an organization or team that needs to change. Conversely, when trust is high, the decision to change begins to feel safer and less threatening. Research shows that when people trust someone, they are more likely to communicate their needs and concerns (reduced resistance) and are also more likely to listen to ideas (increased commitment).[60] The trust that people have for the change leader gets transferred to the change itself. In many ways, the two are inseparable, so change leaders and those who select change leaders need to be mindful of this when evaluating their own performance and making decisions about who should become a change leader. Irrespective of whether your organization is in the beginning, middle, or even final stages of a transformation, maintaining a consistent focus on who the change leaders are and how they are gaining or maintaining credibility is a key factor to monitor to ensure impact.

So how do you achieve the trust and gain credibility needed to achieve change commitment? This is done in two scientifically supported ways. The first is by demonstrating expertise, and the second is through confident communication.

How does it work? A 2004 meta-analysis exploring five decades of studies on persuasiveness and credibility uncovered a consistent link between credibility and expertise.[61] According to cognitive psychologist R. Glen Hass, when the brain recognizes someone as an expert, they are more likely to comply with that person's suggestions. In another infamous laboratory experiment that was turned into a 2015 film, *Experimenter*, the 1960s Milgram Studies is taught in many introductory psychology courses. In the study, volunteer research participants were asked to give clearly labelled electric shocks to a "learner" in a different room who answered the problems incorrectly.[62] The shock levels ranged from mild (a 15-volt slight shock) all the way to danger (severe shock). The learner, who was part of the experiment team, intentionally gave more incorrect answers than correct ones and correspondingly the volunteer "teacher" had to give them a shock. Volunteers could hear the "learners" cries of pain and pleas to stop as the shocks became increasingly worse. If at any point, the teacher refused to give the required shock following an incorrect answer, a lab-coat wearing experimenter (the authoritative expert) would prompt them to follow the instructions and increase the shock level. At the highest level, the learner stopped making any noise at all. Remarkably, the vast majority of the 636 volunteers (65%) administered the highest shock level and all of the participants administered shocks at the 300 volts level.

Stanley Milgram's goal with this experiment was to determine how far an ordinary person would go in following orders given by someone in a position of authority and the answer was clear. Milgram concluded the volunteers were willing to go to such lengths because two conditions were present: 1) the person giving the orders to continue was perceived to be qualified and legitimate (influence factor) and 2) the individuals who administered the shocks believed that authority figure would accept responsibility for the outcome up to and including the death of the learner (trust factor). Such an experiment would not be considered ethical today nor would it be approved to be conducted in an academic setting, but while Milgram's findings carry significant weight from a moral and ethical perspective, it also sheds light on the dynamics of influence and leadership I saw replicated in my own change management research. Namely, that people will at least comply with leaders when they believe those leaders to be credible and legitimate. In short, to increase commitment, change leaders should increase their expertise and ability to speak with credibility and authority on a particular course of action.

Change Mapping

One way to demonstrate expertise and qualify yourself as an expert is by sharing meaningful insights. This can be done by sharing a new idea that aligns to the current or future needs of your organization or creating a fact-based roadmap on a future course of action. Such approaches have a two-fold benefit of helping team members see your vision for the future and demonstrating expertise by outlining a course of action for how that future may be achieved. I call it the change map. A change map may be more or less detailed depending on the culture of your team and, in most cases, it will not detail all (or most) of the action steps needed to achieve the vision but ideally it should represent a visually compelling, 20% future state vision that clearly outlines key vision, goals, timeline, teams, key considerations, and high-level tasks associated with achieving the desired future state. The change map should not be confused with a project charter (e.g., project management) or a detailed change management plan. The change map is a 20% executive-summary style vision of the future that can be presented to a colleague or small team in 5 minutes or less. I have seen many successful executives use this change map approach to take an idea that was in its infancy and shop it around to key stakeholders to gain enough buy-in to take the idea to the next level. The act of creating a change map should not be underestimated because it naturally generates instant credibility for the person who created it by demonstrating you have invested time and mental energy on the change and can present the ideas in a coherent fashion that provides key ideas without being overwhelming.

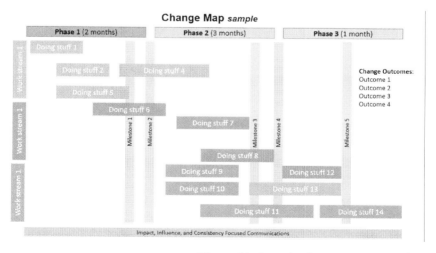

Figure 11. Sample change map template

The second approach for increasing credibility is by displaying confidence. Some have called this executive presence, but the core concept is that confidence has a demonstrable calming effect on the brain.[63] Research shows we are hardwired to place our trust in individuals who display confidence and are leery of people who do not display it. Change leaders can demonstrate confidence by linking past successes to needed future changes. Other ways to increase the credibility quotient include:

1. Share stories of past successes with the proposed change or similar changes
2. Use credibility-enhancing statements such as, "I've been in this industry for twelve years and the transformation our organization needs is not unusual."

Change Influence factor #4: Why Your Change?

Over the past 20 years, organizations have become increasingly matrixed. Employees often have a functional and an operational leader they are responsible to. They also increasingly have dual responsibilities for supporting immediate client needs and managing longer-term projects. In this context, prioritization has more meaning than ever. Highly engaged employees who are committed to doing great work often feel pulled in multiple directions by different leaders and disengaged employees may use this matrixed nature of work to hide behind other priorities. This new reality of work makes selling change even more critical. Unless you are among (and even if you are) the most senior leaders in your organization, smaller change initiatives and even large-scale changes get sold into a noisy workplace of competing priorities and needs. In this context, it can be difficult to be heard, much less gain buy-in to needed changes.

Two rules of cognitive, behavioral, and emotional decision-making undergird this influence factor. These *dominant change motivators* include the desire for gain and the fear of loss. Both need to be leveraged appropriately to foster needed change. The desire for gain refers to the positive outcomes team members will receive during or after the change is complete. In workplaces where the interests of the organization and team members are closely aligned (e.g., senior leaders, organizations with strong shared vision/mission such as the military, or profit-sharing organizations), simply outlining expected organizational benefits such as improved productivity, cost-savings, or additional revenue may suffice for activating the desire for gain. In other organizations, change benefits may need to be outlined in ways that are more aligned to workers' interests, including future career development opportunities, pay increases or bonuses, job security, or schedule flexibility. For example, retail workers may be particularly attuned to organizational change benefits framed as desire for gain because as one recent study found, scheduling flexibility is a particularly strong predictor of retail worker tenure.[64] Retail employees who are provided greater scheduling flexibility showed an increased willingness to stay with their current employer. As an influence factor, change leaders who are able to articulate the benefits of change in terms of expected benefits for those executing the change will have a clear advantage in driving change commitment.

The second dominant change motivator is fear of loss. Researchers have demonstrated fear of loss to be a powerful motivator that can be leveraged in effective and predictable ways to influence behavior and commitment decisions. In a recent 2015 meta-analysis, researchers examining over 127 studies and over 27,000 individuals concluded that fear-based appeals substantially influence attitudes, intentions, and behaviors and that there are very few circumstances under which they are not effective.[65] In addition, the research team identified no circumstances under which fear of loss appeals backfired or led to undesirable outcomes. Those are very compelling research results. Imagine an influence tool so effective it could successfully influence multiple aspects of human behavior and attitudes while having no observable downsides. No doubt Niccolò Machiavelli, who wrote "...it would be best to be both loved and feared. But since the two rarely come together, anyone compelled to choose will find greater security in being feared than in being loved," would feel considerable vindication in such scientific results.[66] As with the Milgram studies, the objective is not to devise ways to inject fear-based practices into the organizational change process, instead, we can use these findings about fear of loss to devise ways to influence change more effectively.

How does it work? There are now decades of research showing that people tend to have stronger feelings about losing something of value than with gaining something of the same value. This tendency is referred to as loss aversion. This means that on the whole, an individual will have a stronger emotional response to losing $5 dollars compared to finding $5 dollars on the ground. Loss aversion theory suggests the desire to avoid losses is wired more strongly into the brain than the desire to achieve gains.[67] While numerous studies have replicated this human propensity on monetary gains and losses, researchers have even replicated this finding in political contexts. When a dispute is framed as jobs being lost versus the possibility of adding jobs, U.S. policymakers were willing to fight harder and hold out longer to prevent an unwanted outcome.[68] Despite these findings, leaders should avoid the temptation to conclude the above research means that to effectively influence change, leaders should frighten or use their positions of power to coerce team members to commit. The key is to balance fear of loss with positive emotions. Overly focusing on fear will lead team members to withdraw emotionally. Indeed, one study of a large-scale restructuring in a public services organization found that negative emotions predicted reduced levels of trust and increased levels of turnover and absenteeism both during the change and 1-month later.[69]

Approach 1: Communicate change benefits in loss terms. Communicate the need for change in ways that tell team members what is at stake and what can be lost if they fail to change, but also discuss the potential benefits of making the change. As discussed in chapter 2, frame benefits in terms of the following benefits:

- Society/Purpose – e.g., building the community and stewarding resources

- Customer – e.g., providing superior service
- Company/Organization – e.g., financial health and shareholder returns
- Working team - e.g., creating a caring and trusting workplace
- Individuals - impact on "me" personally e.g., my development, paycheck, and bonus

Approach 2: maintain the focus on potential loss, not crisis. For any organizational change it can be tempting to create a continuous crisis mode as a tool for attempting to motivate change across their workforce. The challenge with this approach is that it often leads to burnout by creating change fatigue. Even worse, a constant focus on change urgency can foster cynicism in which over time, changes are not taken seriously. The research indicates that messages focused on potential losses taps into a more unlimited motivation pool. This is critical particularly when leading large transformation efforts that have longer-term scope. In those scenarios change leaders will want to tap into a consistent, more sustainable motivational reserves.

Approach 3: Make it easy. This refers to the ability to frame change in ways that are low-cost from a time and effort standpoint. This works best for changes that require relatively low effort in order to produce results. Most team members, especially those who are highly engaged and committed to the vision and mission of the organization, actually want to help and improve the organization if and when they can. In fact research shows that people tend to perceive work as more meaningful when there is a connection between what they do and the well-being of others.[70] By emphasizing how small behavioral changes can have a major impact, change leaders can gain buy-in from those who are already inclined and willing to make small commitments. For example, while leading a change effort to design a new single, internal organization to handle human resources, IT, and finance-related employee and manager questions, we decided to setup the organization so that there was only a single contact point for anyone across the organization requesting services from these functions.

By making it easy and reducing the "cost" of change and showing the impact that changes will have, individuals who are already committed to the organization's or team's success feel free to contribute. Similar to the act of setting up recycle bins next to trash cans, there will always be those who will put everything in the standard trash but most people will at least try to make an effort to recycle if the bins are clearly labelled and easy-to-use. Your job as a change leader is to make it easy for those individuals on your team who are inclined to do the right thing and who want to help despite competing priorities. This is easiest of the approaches, but if you are embarking on a change initiative, consider ways to frame the change in this way--how can change be done in a highly impactful, low-cost, and meaningful way.

Approach 4: Make it matter. When the impact of changing has little visible or tangible results, it becomes easy to ignore. For example, after overhauling its inventory process, a large aerospace manufacturer found that its engineering staff (the top of the proverbial food chain at an aerospace manufacturer) was not using the new process which resulted in long hours and rework by the members of the accounts payable department. Seeing this, the leadership team decided to intervene by setting up an off-site meeting to allow the two groups to interact and give the accounts payable team a chance to show what they did and how their workload was negatively impacted by users who fail to use the new process. Simply by exposing the engineers to the impact their non-use had on their accounts payable colleagues the engineers actually opted to commit to using the new process.

Approach 5: Change Differentiation. Since most changes are introduced into an already change-rich context where a variety of projects, initiatives, and daily work tasks are competing for worker's attention, you need a way to frame your change about what makes it different from the current state or other initiatives that may already be underway. In other words, you have to differentiate the change. For large-scale, transformational changes it may be easier to frame change in this way but for smaller-scale, less impactful or less visible changes, differentiation is vital for gaining the attention needed to drive commitment and behavioral change needed to make the change successful. Differentiation also aligns with the psychological decision-making process. Distinct value refers to the unique value the change initiative will deliver for your organization or your team. It's not uncommon for change leaders to outline this for major initiatives or transformation projects but distinctive value is often deemphasized or not framed in a way that is compelling for workers and team members. Without a clearly articulated distinctive value, the change risks getting deprioritized in the minds of team members. There are two rules for creating a compelling distinctive value.

Rule #1: The distinct value of the change must matter

A common mistake change leaders make when crafting their change management approach, particularly at the executive level, is framing the change around things that matter only to the leadership team. At the individual worker and operational levels, where change initiatives often live or die, if the distinct value of the change is unclear or not viewed as meaningful, most will simply decide to ignore the change or comply based only on fiat (e.g., a senior leader told me I must do this). Neither one of those options is particularly useful in creating meaningful or sustainable change commitment. Distinctive value becomes an influencing factor when it's framed in a way that matters to impacted team members. Chapter 6 illustrates the Build-A-Bear change initiative in detail, but as the current CEO Sharon Price took the helm at the company, she was faced with the challenge of translating Wall Street expectations for improved financial performance into something that was meaningful to the everyday worker at a Build-A-Bear store that you or I might encounter when we enter with our children--no small task. She created distinctive value by starting the 'drive to the dollar' initiative in which all employees would receive a bonus in the event the company successfully achieved a $1 profit. This approach created buy-in across a wide range of employee segments from corporate functions to retail associates and 'builders' by creating a distinct value that mattered.

Price's approach embodied the first rule of change differentiation—she made it matter.

Rule #2: The distinct value must be unique

The second rule is to frame the change in a way that makes it special. The brain has a natural tendency to assign greater value to things that are less easy to obtain (scarcity principle). John F. Kennedy's famous quote encapsulates this idea, "We choose to go to the moon in this decade and do the other things, not because they are easy, but because they are hard." Beyond its inspirational qualities, the speech resonated because as a general rule, the more difficult something is to obtain, the greater its perceived value and the more effort people are willing to exert in achieve it.[71] This effect is true across a range of factors including antiques, time, and toys. As the scarcity of or uniqueness of something is increased, the value also increases so the ability to describe an initiative in a way that is "game-changing" is a way to increase influence potential and commitment.

Application for Change Leaders

A precursor to using change differentiation as an influence factor is framing the change in ways that are meaningful to those impacted. This is done by gaining a detailed understanding of the change context and situation into which the change will be introduced. As you articulate the distinct value (the benefits of the change) to each stakeholder group you are actually helping them through the commitment decision-making process. Examples of ways to frame distinct value include the following:

- How much would it mean for the reputation of ABC, Inc. as a great place to work if we grew our business by 20% over the next year?
- What would a 10% increase in sales mean for your compensation package?

- What would a 15% decrease in line inefficiencies mean for your productivity rate?
- How would we be able to better serve our customers if we were to achieve this change?

In each case, the questions are framed around ideas that are meaningful both to the organization and the workers. These become focal points for dialogue. Effective change leaders know that they need to enlist the commitment of their teams in order to drive sustained commitment even if the outcomes of the change will benefit the organization overall more than individual team members. In some cases, selling change may be easier because there are clear worker-focused benefits, but more often than not, workplace change encompasses areas where the efforts by individual team members will accrue to other teams, departments, or the organization overall. In many cases, leaders simply do not think about ways to frame distinct value in ways that are meaningful to workers and therefore miss a key influence opportunity.

3 steps for applying distinct value:

- Step 1: Understand what matters to your team (what do they care about?)
- Step 2: Identify what is unique and special about your change
- Step 3: Clearly articulate 1 and 2 to your team and, where possible, involve team members in a dialogue around these value focus areas

Bringing it All Together

Throughout this chapter we examined approaches for addressing the four influence factors associated with selling change. These included crafting change messages designed to answer the four questions of:

- Why Change?
- Why Now?

- Why You?
- Why Your Change?

The four change influence factors are powerful change communication metrics you can use to assess how well change is being cascaded throughout your organization. If a critical mass of people are unable to articulate answers to these questions, then your change/transformation effort is in trouble and requires more focused attention to ensure commitment and buy-in levels are high enough to create meaningful shifts in the hearts and minds of your team members.

Chapter 5 - 2IsC™ (Impact, Influence, & Consistency) in Action

"In theory, there is no difference between theory and practice. But in practice, there is."

Yogi Berra

Few things better illustrate a research model better than practical application. In this chapter we examine four major successful or trending towards successful change initiatives. These represent a cross-section of change leaders, industries, and management styles. While unique in their own way, what each of these transformation efforts share is a change management approach that embodies the principles of the 2IsC™ model. This was one of the most exciting parts of writing this book because it demonstrates how effective change leaders sell change in their organization and create successful change outcomes by bringing together the core elements of impact, influence, and consistency. I hope you enjoy these stories as much as I do and can find ways to apply these approaches in your own organization.

Transformation Case Study #1 - Boosting Performance Culture, Rankings, and Financial Health at New York University Langone Medical Center

With its long history of treating patients since 1841 and trifold mission to treat patients, teach, and discover new cutting-edge medical treatments, it seems nearly a foregone conclusion that New York University Langone Medical Center would consistently rank among the top 50 hospitals in the United State and that more than 120 of its physicians would be included in the 2011 list of New York magazine's "Best Doctors."[72] Despite its strong history and established reputation in "the greatest city in the world", less than ten years ago, these results seemed far from attainable for the average physician, nurse, or researcher working at one of center's five-plus hospital, schools, and rehabilitation facilities. The institution was plagued by long-term challenges including eroding market position, declines in quality of care, a fading reputation, and an aging physical infrastructure that threatened to undermine the long-standing health of the medical giant. Enter Robert Grossman, M.D., who became the dean and CEO of the hospital in July 2007.

Beyond the financial and reputational risks, one of the biggest challenges Grossman faced was an intransigent culture characterized by an entrenched and entitled staff in the institution's academic medical center. Four months into his tenure, Grossman introduced a bold, clear-eyed 10-year vision to return NYU Langone to its status as a "world-class, patient-centered integrated academic medical center." This phrase was straight out of a CEO transformation playbook—one of those high-minded visions that sounds great to shareholders and the board but also gives workers and staff an eye-roll moment.

> "...NYU Langone's transformation has had people at its core. I knew that a more committed, engaged workforce would be the primary element of competition in a service-driven, knowledge-intensive business such as healthcare."
>
> -Robert Grossman, M.D.,
> CEO NYU Langone

The impact of what Grossman was proposing should not be underestimated. Here is why. The gap between the then current state of NYU Langone's operations and Grossman's future vision was significant. The School of Medicine was losing more than $12 million each month and not making that up in revenue. His use of the term "integrated" signaled his expectation that collaboration, resources, and missions would need to become more integrated across research, education, and clinical care. His use of the term "world-class" portended a new era of externally validated standards and the possibility for comparisons to other well-known and established medical, research, and teaching institutions including Harvard, the University of Pennsylvania, and Johns Hopkins. The impact of what Grossman was proposing would hit the organization like a sledgehammer. He put it best, "I wanted to articulate the vision early and let people know I meant it."

Creating a broad-based future vision

Though adopting a decisive approach by creating a clear 1-page "50,000-foot" vision (see chapter 5) for the future direction of the institution overall, Grossman also maintained the principles of 2IsC™ change management by engaging his top team in a participatory fashion to draft a "10,000-foot" vision of the proposed change plan in which they detailed how their respective departments and functions would align to the new vision. He further engaged his team by establishing bi-weekly meetings designed to breakdown silos, encourage collaboration, and examine possible areas of integration. By creating joint management and executive-level responsibility between the medical school and the hospital, Grossman created an environment in which challenges no longer fell under the purview of one area or the other but instead each shared joint responsibility for outcomes. Interestingly, Grossman and his team opted to start with the "back office" functions of IT, HR, real estate, and facilities - operating under the assumption that by coordinating efforts among functional areas without direct client touchpoints, NYU Langone would be able to demonstrate what was possible and start to gain traction for front-line patient services. This approach increased the impact quotient and reduced possible resistance from detractors who might have been inclined to say cross-function and departmental coordination was not possible.

About a year after engaging top leaders, Grossman broadened the scope of the transformative engagement efforts to include more than 500 leaders whom he convened to discuss the institution's future. Over the course of four large-group meetings, leaders discussed their

> **"Other people began to say we could be a great institution. We had awakened their imagination to the possibilities."**
>
> -Robert Grossman, M.D., CEO NYU Langone

progress against the plans already in put in place, including record-breaking fundraising results as well as their visions for the future. People were glad to discuss the impacts they were having and in so doing created forward momentum. By bringing this group together, Grossman embodied the 'consistency' factor of the 2IsC™ model demonstrating how persistence and continued effort maintains and reinvigorates team members' energy towards transformation efforts.

A data-driven change approach

As transformation efforts continued, Grossman adopted a uniquely engaging data-driven approach. As scientists, researchers, and physicians, many of the core staff at NYU Langone were no strangers to using data and evidence to make critical patient decisions and advance medical breakthroughs. However, as an institution, many had moved away from using similar, data-driven approaches to measuring functional and departmental effectiveness. Grossman challenged his leadership team to define "world-class, patient-centered integrated academic medical center" performance metrics at the frontlines of delivery for each functional area. After defining these, the team created a web-based dashboard that was initially only visible to the top leadership, including Grossman himself, and the vice deans. Grossman considered this dashboard a "single source of truth" which he later made visible to all the department chairs.

> **"I was able to look at data every day from my office and know what was happening throughout the institution. It did not take long, and soon others were looking as well and making improvements in their own departments as well as learning from others."**
>
> -Robert Grossman, M.D., CEO NYU Langone

The performance dashboard tool served a tri-fold purpose as an impact, influence, and consistency tool by showing each departmental leader how they were doing (impact), allowing them to compare their department's performance results (influence), and driving behaviors that would align to the long-term vision of the institution (consistency). What's more, departmental leaders were able to assess their own progress using metrics and corresponding data that they had helped define. This both drove and created an environment for a culture of information and participation-based change leadership approaches to thrive. This data-driven approach was also crucial for driving production discussions with physicians in the institution's hospital system. The data created a standardized assessment environment where even the most well-regarded and productive clinicians could be held accountable for the results they were producing.

Managing deeper organizational issues

One of the things that makes transformation efforts challenging and why there is often so much resistance stems from the fact that there are many long-term team members who have gotten used to current or past practices. This was certainly the case at NYU Langone. In his push to move the medical center back to the top of the research field, Grossman and the change leaders had to address several long-standing practices and structural barriers. One of these was a practice common in many organizations--many of the institution's leaders had been promoted on the basis of their performance as individual researchers or clinicians rather than their strength as effective organizational leaders managing people, financial, and operational resources. What's more, they had not adequately developed those skills during their time in leadership positions resulting in leaders who had control over large segments of the medical center's resources but limited effectiveness in delivering the results the institution needed to be effective. Grossman knew this was an entrenched organizational barrier and he would need board of director support to tackle this issue.

Prior to taking a multi-pronged approach of creating term limits for chair positions, establishing clear performance expectations for leadership, and restructuring the leadership scope, he first got support from board to make these changes. This preemptively stopped tenured leaders who tried to go to the board from getting around the higher leadership and role expectations. By 2015, 30 out of the 33 department chairs had been replaced. Some were voluntary, as they saw the handwriting on the proverbial wall and opted for early retirement or buy-out plans instead, while some of these moves were involuntary, and yet others adapted (the 3 who remained) and began allocating resources in ways to support increased productivity expectations.

Consistency at Work

Grossman and the board's moves to make hard decisions about restructuring NYU Langone to align to the transformation efforts underscored two important points that get to the heart of the consistency factor of the 2IsC™ model. The first is that sometimes, but not always, good intentions, information-based change leadership strategies, a clear vision, role-modeling, and engagement-focused actions will not be enough to drive commitment across all stakeholders. There are some transformation efforts that are so significant and may violate too many of the needs in the hierarchy that some team members will simply not be willing or able to get onboard with the new ways of doing things. This is where the principle of consistency gets tested. In NYU Langone's case, consistency took two key forms. The first was Grossman's efforts to create a culture of accountability at the leadership level by increasing standards and gaining board commitment by ensuring there were no backdoor channels to get around those higher performance expectations. The second was by highlighting and championing gains from the new approach. He did so by emphasizing early wins and successes in winning grants,

> **"We needed to convince the great majority in the middle that they would actually benefit from meeting the higher expectations of a top-performing institution."**
>
> -Robert Grossman, M.D.,
> CEO NYU Langone

providing additional financial resources, and improving rankings - all of which contributed to growing support. This provided the proof that the vision for NYU Langone was possible and achievable. This also created a degree of trust that NYU Langone's management was serious about transforming into a new vision of itself for its patients and the research community it contributed to.

Proof of Change

The fruits of Grossman's approach have been undeniable. Overall revenues have more than tripled, the hospital now consistently receives five stars for overall performance, and it is ranked by U.S. News & World Report as one of the 10 best hospitals in the U.S. And what about the medical school and hospitals that was initially beset

> **"I knew that if I tried to dictate changes from above, the effort would backfire, undermining morale and productivity. But if I was too passive, the company would simply continue its downward spiral."**
>
> -Robert Grossman, M.D., CEO NYU Langone

by so much infighting? NYU Langone's hospitals have received top rankings for overall patient safety and quality of care for four years straight and the medical school has risen in U.S. News and World Report's rankings from 34 to 11 in seven years — one of the more rapid increases in the magazine's history. Research grant funding from the National Institutes of Health (NIH) rose from $122 million in 2008 to $189 million in 2016, despite NIH funding remaining virtually flat nationally.[73] Beyond the numbers, NYU Langone Medical tops the list of transformational change selling cases because the leadership team had to embody each of the 2IsC™ principles to sell change across the medical center's disparate operations and execute on each dimension of Impact, Influence, and Consistency. The leadership team's consistent focus on selling change, by co-creating impact-oriented stories and using participation and information-based change leadership to drive transformations enabled the medical institution to transform itself.

Transformation Case Study #2 - Creating Manufacturing Capacity at Nissan

The year was 1999 and Renault had just ended its search for a manufacturing partner when then CEO, Louis Schweitzer, placed the call to Carlos Ghosn requesting whether he was willing to take the reins at Nissan. Similar to the situation Robert Grossman walked into at NYU Langone, Nissan was a former auto powerhouse that found itself in tough times. Analysts estimated that Nissan lost $1,000 for every car it sold in the U.S., the Japanese plants were overcapacity (producing more than a million more cars a year than the company sold), and the company was more than $11 billion in debt.[74] Nissan had been attempting to become profitable for the previous 8 years with limited success. The merger would turn the combined company into the world's fourth largest carmaker. Both parties believed the complementarity of Renaults' innovative design and cash reserves could be combined with Nissan's engineering capabilities and North American market presence to build a stronger company together. At the strategy level, this seemed like a win-win, but it would require serious effort to make this vision a reality.

> **Commitment to cost reductions**
>
> When the CEO suggested Nissan could reduce supplier costs by 20% to bring the company in line with other auto manufacturers, the company's engineers scoffed. Nissan's core competency was engineering and their specifications were already tougher than many of their competitors. So what did the CEO do? He outsourced it to a cross-functional team (Influence factor). Under the leadership of a cross-functional management structure that had absolutely no decision-making authority, a team of engineers figured out a way to modify headlamp reflectors to reduce both the rejection rate (quality) and the cost of headlamps, decreasing the costs of production on headlamps alone by 2.5%. The same engineers who thought it was impossible, made the impossible a reality by using only Impact and the Influence factor of Participation-based Change leadership.

In less than three years, Nissan had become profitable and boosted its brand. How? Ghosn attributes Nissan's success to two factors that align almost perfectly with the 2IsC™ approach. The first was setting up cross-functional teams to identify changes that needed to be made (participation-based change leadership + impact). The second was giving the company room to build on the best elements of itself (trust).

What they did

Ghosn opted to make the establishment of cross-functional teams the centerpiece of Nissan's transformation efforts. This direction was not dissimilar from Grossman at NYU Langone, who began their transformation with a focus on cross-functional alignment across the support functions of HR, IT, and Finance. At Nissan, Ghosn saw these cross-functional teams as the key ingredient in getting line managers to think about the organization beyond their immediate functional and regional boundaries. In short, he saw cross-functional teams as a way of reframing problems. This provided lower-level managers with a perspective on managing their teams that was more closely aligned to how executive leadership saw the organization. Managers who primarily lead within functional boundaries have limited perspective in providing approaches needed to unify separate work activities and work streams into an integrated whole. Ghosn put it best when he said, "...working together in cross-functional teams helps managers to think in new ways and challenge existing practices. The teams also provide a mechanism for explaining the necessity for change and for projecting difficult messages across the entire company."[75] Ghosn's approach to using cross functional teams allowed him to leverage the power of Impact and Influence. Impact by demonstrating the seriousness and meaningfulness of the new approach by redesigning the company to operate in a fundamentally different way than it had done so previously, and Influence by allowing leaders to participate in crafting a new approach to achieving company results.

Nearly a month after arriving at Nissan, Ghosn had established nine cross-functional teams to directly address key drivers of Nissan's performance. Interestingly, although the cross-functional teams had no decision-making power, they were granted "full access" to all information about the company operations—talk about rapid, agile change. Even more interesting, this group of 10 members had been identified from the ranks of middle management. The thinking was that this hand-picked group would have the ear of the executives as well as enough on-the-ground experience to know what was feasible and deliver real results. From a capacity perspective, each cross-functional team manager was able to create a set of sub teams who could "deep dive" and create recommendations on issues that required more time to craft solutions.

These groups came together to create the Nissan Revival Plan that included a range of objectives Nissan needed to achieve, including launching 22 models, improving capacity utilization from 53% to 82%, reducing SG&A costs by 20%, and reducing variation in parts by 50%. The groups were given 3 months to review the company's operations and come up with recommendations for returning Nissan to profitability while also devising opportunities for future growth.

In addition to creating a high-impact plan that leveraged core elements of the 2IsC™ model including information-based change leadership (e.g., the revival plan) and participation-based change leadership (e.g., setting up cross-functional teams), Ghosn also fostered an environment of trust. He set exceptionally high standards for reporting and applied those standards equally to himself and his team. Because so much of Nissan's revival plan was based on accurate performance data and reporting, Ghosn only accepted reports that had clear and verifiable numbers. In return, he put himself on the line declaring that he would resign if the company failed to meet any of the commitments that were agreed upon and set. This created an atmosphere of trust that signaled to every worker that the top-most leader was taking the transformation effort seriously and was willing to put himself on the line to the same degree he was asking everyone else to.

In February of 2017, it was announced that Ghosn would be stepping down as Nissan's CEO, but he is credited with bringing the auto-manufacturer back from the brink of financial ruin.[76]

> **"We had the trust of employees for a simple reason: We had shown them respect."**
>
> -Carlos Ghosn, CEO, Nissan

Like Grossman, Ghosn was known for cost-cutting but he did not stop there. He attributes this successful turnaround at Nissan to the formation of cross-functional teams (Impact + Influence factors – participation-based leadership) and his willingness to allow Nissan's employees, "...to develop a new corporate culture," (Consistency – trust). Many organizational leaders use sports as a metaphor for illustrating how groups of people work together to create wins. An avid Formula One racing fan, Ghosn was no different. To achieve the highest levels of performance, he stated that racers must, "... accelerate, brake, and accelerate all the time. The revival plan, therefore, was as much about future growth (accelerating) as it was about cutting costs (braking). We couldn't say, 'There will be a time for cost reduction and then a time for growth'—we had to do both at once."

The story of Nissan's transformation was extraordinary not only in terms of the ability of an outside leader to quickly gain the buy-in and commitment from a cross-section of workers spanning disparate countries and cultures. It was also compelling in terms of its speed. This was one of the original "agile" cross-organizational transformations that was enabled by bringing together a cross-section of workers and creating cross-functional teams that allowed them to provide their inputs and co-create stories of future success using a high-trust approach.

Transformation Case Study #3 - Building Buy-In at Build-A-Bear

> "Failure is an extraordinary catalyst for change."
>
> -Sharon Price, CEO Build A Bear

Build-A-Bear Workshop, Inc. is one of retail's most beloved companies. Walk by a Build-A-Bear in your local mall at peak time and peer inside. You would be hard-pressed not to smile as you hear the giggles from children and watch the bustle of activity from the store workers as they work to create the perfect stuffed bear to meet the exact specifications of one of the many eager children lined up to take their prized bear home.

Build-A-Bear has been expanding rapidly since it opened its first store in 1997 in St Louis Missouri.[77] It's even made Fortune's list of 100 Best Workplaces for more than 5 years in a row. With such excitement surrounding such a popular brand with a value proposition that no one could argue with--customized stuffed bears for children—one might be surprised to learn the company was hemorrhaging money. In 2012, the company reported a net loss of $49 million.[78] The prior CEO, Maxine Clark, was on her way out but had set the groundwork for a possible turnaround. That foundation had all the hallmarks of a classic change approach which included closing non-profitable stores (downsizing) and updating marketing/brand messaging and store design (increase revenue by making the stores more appealing). While not bad, this MBA-style approach was likely to make Wall Street investors happy but certainly was not going to fill employees who would be living through and bearing responsibility for executing this strategy with feelings of warmth or engagement, much less commitment to the changes needed to make the turnaround possible. Enter the new CEO Sharon Price.

Starting with a core value and common practice

Out of the gate, Price launched into her role by talking about what's known in Build-A-Bear as the 'heart ceremony'. This is the point in the process of building a bear where a person (usually a child) puts a heart into their new bear. It is not hard to imagine this being an emotionally poignant moment for both the new bear owner and the Build-a-Bear staff who are there to witness it. As Build-A-Bear's new leader, Price thought long and hard about how to turnaround this iconic brand and kept coming back to the heart ceremony. She went on to devise a two-fold company-wide change approach consisting of 1) "Drive to the Dollar" and 2) "The Gumby Effect". Under 'Drive to the Dollar' Sharon implored the company to work towards achieving a $1 dollar profit target. Despite the almost laughable profitability target, this was no small feat for an organization that had not made money in over 3 years. Sharon promised that if the company made at least $1 in profit, all employees would receive a bonus. The Gumby Effect is a reference to a Gumby costume Price kept on-hand to playfully remind company team members to avoid reverting back to old habits and maintain their focus on flexibility and results.[79]

"...see the vision and see how we can be more!"

-Sharon Price, CEO Build-A-Bear

Under her leadership, Price took the company from a $49 million loss to a $14 million dollar gain in her first year. While Build-A-Bear has yet to fully realize its planned goals and growth targets, this story of a stuffed bear turnaround highlights the simplistic genius of Price's approach to gaining the type of commitment needed to turn a net loser into a net gainer in less than one year. Firstly, Price began with a fundamental understanding that her team and employees were essential to making the progress she and Build-A-Bear's investors needed. Beyond the numbers and an admittedly strong brand, Price understood that change was not likely to happen without a core base of employees supporting it who were themselves also committed to making and supporting that change. To drive impactful buy-in and commitment at the employee level, the Drive to the Dollar approach provided a direct, yet easily identifiable target for employees to get behind. No doubt most in the company were well aware the company was underwater financially and were willing to support efforts to turn things around but just needed direction and a first step.

Achieving a profitability target of $1 represented a way to do that. It was general enough for everyone from the marketing department to the retail store employee to get behind and was also empowering in that everyone could see their role in achieving the goal. In fact, Price has spoken about how she would overhear unwitting employees conversing with each other about how to reduce expenses saying, "Don't buy that. We can do this instead. Don't spend my bonus!" The management team even setup a virtual suggestion box where people could send their ideas and suggestions on ways to reduce costs and increase revenues across the company. Sharon Price's success at driving employee commitment and buy-in to a massive turnaround effort at Build-A-Bear embodies the core concept of this book. When team members understand the impact of change, are equipped with the right kinds of information about the change, and perceive consistent behavior coming from individuals responsible for leading the change effort, they are more likely to be fully committed to the change. This effect is not just anecdotal, it is supported by cross-industry, academic research. In short, Impact + Influence + Consistency = Full Commitment.

How it works

When Sharon Price announced the Drive to the Dollar plan, she tapped into the first and most predictive principle of employee commitment and that is impact. Impact refers to how

> "Workers would tell each other, "Don't buy that. We can do this instead. Don't spend my bonus!"
>
> -Sharon Price, CEO Build A Bear

significant the change is perceived to be. Overall, research shows change impact to be the biggest contributing factor to employees' level of commitment to change. In other words, you can determine how much someone will be committed to a change in their workplace simply by knowing how impactful they believe the change to be.

By adopting a change approach that tapped directly into an aspect of the workplace that impacts every employee (their pay), Price tapped into the single largest driver of employee commitment. Price linked her vision of a company turnaround to something every employee had some level of control over. Many books and articles focus on leadership with a capital "L" often referring to the senior leadership team, but often, little attention is paid to the small "l" leaders that make every organization operate on a daily and weekly basis. In her research on retail employees, Zeynep Ton details the countless decisions retail store workers make on a minute-by-minute basis (see *Why commitment counts especially in retail*). These decisions are a key factor, particularly in the retail industry where profit margins are low.

When Price created a change platform that was broad, yet also personally impactful, she produced a turnaround approach that increased the impact quotient across Build-A-Bear's nearly 6,000 employees and initiated a multiplier effect for decisions each employee could make about their own individual work decisions and customer interactions. This should not be underestimated. Employees who buy-in to change figuratively extend the reach of the organization's leader or leadership team's vision. As Price herself witnessed, Build-A-Bear staff who were committed to the turnaround strategy, or at least committed to getting a bonus, actually governed themselves and their co-workers in support of the new approach.

At this point, one might be tempted to view this as primarily a compensation issue—e.g., employees wanted a bonus so they did what they could to get it. However, the concept of impact extends beyond pay. In strange twist, behavioral research shows that employees will commit to changes in their organization even if they do not agree with the change.[80] As long as they perceive the impact of the change to be high enough, they will demonstrate a willingness to commit almost solely on this basis alone.

Beyond impact, there is another factor that is predictive of change commitment and that is influence. Influence includes a range of factors but at the core of influence is the type of change leadership strategy used to execute change. Of the three types of change leadership strategies assessed, information-based change leadership strategy was the second strongest predictor of employees' commitment to change (after impact). Information-based strategies use reason and logic to motivate team members to change. Under this approach, change leaders create a "business case" for change where they work to provide information to their teams that justifies and legitimizes the change. As outlined in chapter 4, effective information-based change leadership occurs when leaders provide team members with clarity about the process and the goals and legitimate reasons for the change are clearly established.

One of the reasons why information is so important is because change can be scary. Not only in the sense that jobs may be at risk (although that is a significant factor as well) but also because of what change represents. At its core, change means letting go of something old and adopting, adapting to, or even creating something new and anything new is, by definition, unpredictable and unknown and will create some level of anxiety. While there is a percentage of the population who are "change agents" and advanced thinkers who are ahead of their time and ready to jump into the great unknown with both feet, most people tend to be a bit more hesitant about making changes, big or small. Generally, when people feel they have something of value to lose, information-based change leadership plays an outsized role in the commitment journey.[81] By creating a strong case for change and setting a clear vision for the future, change leaders are in effect, reducing the mental and emotional risks associated with taking the risk to do something new.

In Build-A-Bear's case, Price embodied the principle of influence by telling employees about her plan to grow the company into a larger enterprise beyond retail. She explained that Build-A–Bear was a brand that was more than the retail stores and that in the future, the retail stores would be one of several revenue streams for the company. While her vision for the future of the company is easily open to interpretation, debate, and both optimism and cynicism depending on where one sits in the organization, the emphasis here is on the fact that she was able to speak to a clear vision and plan which she laid out for Build-A-Bear's employees and satisfied the employees' need for information. As was the case with impact, the focus is less about whether workers view the change as positive or negative, and more about whether the change is something that provides enough information to drive commitment. Often, change leaders get caught-up in the perceived impact of the change (e.g., the employees won't like this direction or they will resist) but research on organizational change suggests that lack of impact and inadequate information represent larger challenges when it comes to gaining employee buy-in.

Sharon Price's participation-based approach was embodied by her penchant for informally asking questions and her belief in the principle of 'management by walking around'.[82] Price is known for making surprise store visits and simply talking to her team members about how things are going. While a less formal means of involving employees, it accomplishes the same thing. Chapter 4 explores participation-based change leadership in more detail including formal and informal ways change leaders can use participation as a tool to drive employee commitment.

Build-A-Bear, like most organizations, is still a work in progress. After an incredible 3 years of positive growth that nearly tripled its stock price 220%, the company hit a rough patch during the December 2016 holiday season when it posted a fourth quarter loss.[83] Despite the short-term setback, which is inevitable in almost any organizational context, Price has laid the groundwork for sustainable long-term growth at an organization that exists in a difficult-to-occupy market niche. She did this by 'selling change' using impact, influence, and consistency

A Toys R Us Kid

As of the writing of this book, Toys R Us recently announced its plans to close/sell its U.S. stores, as well as the death of its founder. As a kid I remember it being one of the most exciting places to visit, right up there with Chuck E Cheese and Disney World. As an adult, it was interesting to consider the juxtaposition between Toys R Us and Build-A-Bear. The classic fall-from-success storyline was that Toys R Us simply couldn't compete against the likes of large, big-box discounters such as Walmart and or its web-based nemesis, Amazon.com. However, despite similar financial headwinds, Build-A-Build seems to be weathering the storm. I believe this is due to Build-A-Bear's intentional focus on including employees and staff in its turnaround efforts. In fact, Toys R Us' CEO seemed to concur. In its 2017 fall financial filings, the company indicated it was planning spend $72 million between 2018 and 2021 to raise its wages to reward and keep its most effective employees in order to create an engaging, customer-focused store experience that Build-A-Bear seems to have mastered. However, this proved to be too little, too late for this once powerful toy store. As Toys R Us CEO, David Brandon put it, "Better employees make for happier customers." Price knew this and used it to Build-A-Bear's advantage to transform the organization and grow its success.

Transformation Case Study #4 - Turning it Around at Chipotle with Trust & Consistency

After graduating from the Culinary Institute of America, Steve Ells began working in a San Francisco-based restaurant called Stars. He always had a dream of starting his own restaurant, but how or what it would be did not occur to him until he was sitting in small taqueria.[84] As he watched the workers preparing and serving the various burrito and enchilada dishes, Ells was inspired by how the restaurant was able to make inexpensive food with fresh ingredients. Ells remembers, "I took out a napkin and jotted down what I thought the average check was and how many people were going through the line, and I timed it. I thought, Wow, this thing makes a lot of money -- it could be a little cash cow that could fund my real restaurant." After getting an $85,000 family loan, Ells proceeded to open the first Chipotle restaurant in 1993.

Fall from Fast-Casual Heaven

Many in the U.S. are familiar with the unique taste and healthy portion sizes of a Chipotle burrito and, for the health-conscious, the burrito bowl. However, Chipotle's meteoritic rise to the top of the fast-causal food chain phenomenon nearly ended when a series of food-poisoning incidents in multiple locations across the entire country occurred in early 2016. In total, more than 500 people became sick with several food-borne illnesses including E. coli, norovirus, and salmonella after eating at Chipotle restaurants.[85] The outbreaks spanned as far as California, Illinois, Maryland, Ohio, Pennsylvania and Washington. Despite a Center for Disease Control (CDC) investigation showing the cases were not connected, for a household brand like Chipotle that markets its cleanliness and quality, the damage had already been done.

The response

Beyond simply making a series of apologies and promises to rectify the situation in any way it could, Chipotle's leadership took the very visible step of closing all 2,250 of its locations for a 4-hour period while the company's leadership sought answers from its nearly 60,000+ employees on ways to make operational changes (participation-based leadership) and provide the opportunity for a question and answer session (information-based leadership). Chipotles' leadership team also thanked and acknowledged team members for their hard work. The company also undertook an investigation to find out the source of the outbreaks and traced a norovirus outbreak in Virginia to an employee who was working while sick.[86] In response, Chipotle increased its communication and training efforts. Several 2IsC™ takeaways from Chipotle's response included:

- Being open and honest about the problems that plagued the company
- Identifying the root cause of the problems and having an open and honest dialogue about what happened and what to do about it (not hiding or suppressing the issue)
- Visibly taking time out to show how seriously company leadership took this issue (closing all stores for 4 hours)
- Conducting training and setting clear expectations about what was needed
- Recognizing and rewarding the behaviors they wanted to see repeated.

On the customer side, company leadership gave away free entrees to anyone who claimed to have had their lunch plans derailed. This too was a trust-creating exercise in that they were not forcing patrons to prove they had been impacted—they took their word for it. A message that no doubt communicated a powerful trust message internally as well.

Road to recovery

As of the writing of this, Chipotle has yet to return to its pre-fall status from a customer and financial perspective. It continues to face fallout from previous outbreaks and remains under the microscope for news.[87] However, analysts are projecting its high share price to be nearly double that of its lowest projected price. This burrito giant seems well-positioned for growth and this in major part due to its approach to selling change in the midst of crisis.

Transformation Case Study #5 - Transforming a Silicon Valley Operating Model

A company that began as a college project has turned into one of Silicon Valley's success stories.[88] Box.com (formerly Box.net) is operating in an incredibly challenging and competitive high-tech marketplace with the likes of Google Drive, Dropbox, and Microsoft OneDrive in the marketplace of cloud-based file-sharing. Despite this, the company has taken a decidedly measured pace to transforming its operations. The company's leadership discovered the one of the secrets to effective organizational change is to move slower (not faster). Since dropping out of college 12 years ago to start Box, CEO Aaron Levie has turned down a buy-out offer of $600 million dollars, grown the company from a small core of 15 employees to over 6,500 globally, and pivoted the company from primarily a consumer-focused business to more business/enterprise-focused offerings.[89]

"Because if you come in every week or every month or every quarter where you're pivoting the company, you're not going to be able to maintain an aligned, high-executing, high-functioning workforce and organization, and so you do have to be thoughtful about those big moments."

-Aaron Levie, CEO, Box

The changes at Box necessitated a change in its approach to managing change. The transition to focus on enterprise software offerings meant that Box needed to become more disciplined in its approach to when and how to focus its resources and efforts. Levie observed that the company's lack of discipline and focus made it difficult for the company to focus on its priorities. The key message being that when it comes to organizational change, less is often-times more. By identifying a clear long-term strategy and vision of what the company wanted to be and then working backwards, Box's leadership team was better able to identify the core projects, initiatives, and change activities that needed to occur in the near-term to support that strategy.

Aligning people to new product offerings – Democratizing Innovation

In 2016, discussions on the subjects of machine learning and artificial intelligence (AI) and its implications for Box began to emerge within the company. Internally, Box already had an approach to tackling new software development through hackathons held every six months. The engineering team had already begun creating some new AI capabilities but nothing had yet materialized into real offerings. The Box team put together a working group comprised of resources and team members representing a cross-section of team members on the engineering team. They setup weekly meetings to discuss the impacts machine learning and AI could have on their product offerings. Before long, Box created a formal team to look into the capabilities and began shifting people to work on it on a full-time basis. Although the entire process has taken more than a year, by allocating resources, Box has positioned itself to bring newer, more innovative capabilities to its customer base by leveraging the following five innovation and growth-focused steps:

1. Creating a clear direction for future-focused capabilities
2. Allocating adequate financial, time, and people resources to tackle desired capabilities
3. Democratizing the change process (participation change leadership) to allow the best and brightest to craft ideas and solutions to carry the innovation process forward
4. Build trust by making it okay to make mistakes
5. Allowing adequate time to build required innovative product and offerings.

Levie and the leadership team at Box embodied the principles of influence and consistency focused change leadership by emphasizing the participation-based change leadership and creating a trust-based culture. Levie admitted that when the team first began its work, there were missteps in the execution of AI. Rather than throwing in the towel, the leadership team gave their engineers the time and space they needed to learn from these mistakes and over time, they expanded their core capabilities in this new space. Instead of giving up, the Box team doubled-down on their efforts but did so in increasingly smarter ways that eliminated elements of new product innovation that would not work and focusing on and increasing investments in areas and people who would pay-off in the long-run. In so doing, Box became an exemplar in selling enterprise software and organizational change effectiveness.

Bringing it all together

Whether a culture transformation across a distributed medical/ research institution, reducing expenses while streamlining manufacturing processes and innovation at an auto manufacturer, overhauling the customer experience while returning to profitability in the retail sector, or creating innovative, enterprise software offerings, each of the change leaders in this chapter led their organizations through significant transformation efforts. They each did so through a combination of communications and behaviors centered on selling change (impact) and then leading those changes using influence and consistency. Each of these case studies illustrate the importance of leading with Impact, Influence, and Consistency. Using these elements to "sell" change to their teams, leaders at these organizations reaped the benefits of committed change, including higher levels of worker performance and team members who were more willing to learn new skills and behaviors. But, most importantly, these organizations ultimately showed higher rates of change and transformation success. Together these represent the holy grail of organizational transformation.

Chapter 6 - Creating an Outcomes-Focused Change Strategy

"Organizations don't execute unless the right people, individually and collectively, focus on the right details at the right time."

Ram Charan, *author,* Execution: The Discipline of Getting Things Done

Effective leadership is not about "managing" the change process but instead adopting an effective change leadership strategy that improves the way change is 'sold' to team members and that will get them to engage in the process of doing things in a different way. It may require revisiting your change management model, but the most important change is transforming your approach to influencing stakeholders across the organization.

Traditionally, change managers were expected to put together communication plans, identify stakeholders, and improve the overall process for changing the behavior of individuals across the organization. Today, change leaders need the ability to "sell" the need for change across multiple stakeholder groups who often have interests that do not (easily) align. This means mastering the ability to talk about change initiatives in ways that address these questions:

- How does the change align to the value your organization provides?
- How will the change create value for the people who rely on your organization (internal and external)?
- Why should stakeholders from different parts of the organization work towards the change goals?

- How will the change enable the organization to balance customer/stakeholder relationships and internal stakeholders to ensure sustainable growth and organizational success?

Transforming your organization requires challenging some underlying core assumptions. It requires recognizing blind spots and formulating ways to think differently about every aspect of your organization's operations—customers, team members, data, innovation, and value. Much like Nissan's move towards a streamlined decision-making and leadership model, it is possible for large organizations that might otherwise seem insular and 'stuck in their ways' to revamp their entire way of working and operating.

So why aren't more organizations able to accomplish this? The fact is that for every Nissan or NYU Langone Medical Center that succeeds in transforming their operations, there is a Blockbuster, RadioShack, or Toys R Us that fails. Why is it so difficult to adapt and keep up? One of the key reasons is lack of focus on outcomes-focused organizational change. It is not enough to recognize the need for organizational change or transformation—or even to understand how the principles of effective change leadership apply to your own industry and organization. Leaders at successful legacy organizations must be ready to make change happen at a rapid pace and across a wide range of stakeholder groups. The size and scale of large organizations compound this issue through sheer volume of stakeholders, decision-makers, and divergent interests that need to be aligned. These layers can become "speed bumps" that, if not addressed, can slow-down and hold-off future change efforts. To sell organizational change in this operating environment, change leaders need to focus on Impact, Influence, and Consistent.

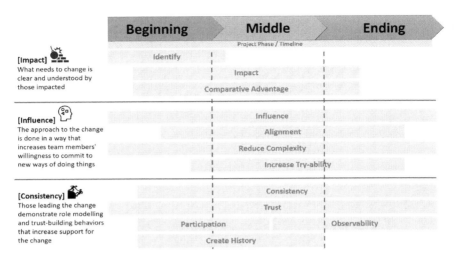

	Beginning	Middle	Ending
	Project Phase / Timeline		
[Impact] What needs to change is clear and understood by those impacted	Identify	Impact	
		Comparative Advantage	
[Influence] The approach to the change is done in a way that increases team members' willingness to commit to new ways of doing things		Influence	
		Alignment	
		Reduce Complexity	
		Increase Try-ability	
[Consistency] Those leading the change demonstrate role modelling and trust-building behaviors that increase support for the change		Consistency	
		Trust	
	Participation		Observability
	Create History		

Figure 12. 2IsC™ across 3 project phases

Here's how:

Impact: How do we communicate the importance and relevance of needed changes? What needs to change is clear and understood by those who are impacted.

1. **Identify Impact:** Explain what the change(s) are and what it means for who and what the organization will be and do in the future. Demonstrate the consequences if no changes are made (e.g., loss of customers, declining reputation, job losses, etc.)

2. **Leverage Emotions:** Research shows that emotions tell us what's important and where to focus our energy and attention. Emotions, whether positive or negative, are the frames by which our minds filter what is important versus not. Use stories to convey emotions and craft change messages about what organizational changes will mean for your organization and team as well as customers and constituents. For example, insurance companies leverage the imagery of family and home to sell otherwise static, infrequently-used, financial instruments.

3. **Impact:** Articulate the importance of the change and what the effect will be on team members, jobs, work tasks, and future success.

4. **Simplify:** People tend to simplify things, especially topics that are complex, because it makes things easier to deal with and process mentally. When a change is perceived to be complex and convoluted (even if it actually is), many team members will simply "check-out" unless they absolutely have to be involved in the process—that is "have-to" commitment and not the ideal type of "want-to" commitment change leaders need to engender to be successful.

5. **Focus on what's most important:** The most important aspects of the change include the results and expected outcomes. Effective change leaders know the further they move away from these, the harder it becomes to maintain change commitment and motivation.
6. **Comparative Advantage:** Present ways change will provide more benefits or better results compared to the current ways of doing things.
7. **Avoid the tendency for "information overload":** While research shows that timely and relevant information and information-based change leadership is critical to getting team members to buy-in and commit, too much information will make the change seem overly complex and not worth the effort.
8. **Make it easily digestible:** Make sure there is an easily digestible 'helicopter' or 'high-level' version of change communications available in the change 'pitch' or change proposal—think 'what's the 30-second version' of this change?

Influence: How do we align our leadership and stakeholders around required changes? The approach to the change is done in a way that increases team members' willingness to commit to new ways of doing things.

1. **Self-Concept:** The initiatives team members opt to commit themselves to are often reflections of who they are and who they aspire to be. Part of the change leader's job is to sell change by making leaders and team members who are involved in the change process look good by outlining ways in which the change initiative will help them become their ideal selves and an ideal organization. Research on employee

engagement shows that everyone wants to be part of a winning team and engagement levels increase when people believe they are, irrespective of other management activities.

2. **Assess the Change Climate:** Conduct a stakeholder assessment to identify impacts, training, and communication needs based on the type of change.

3. **Align Leadership & Stakeholders:** Match the leadership approach to the type of change and attitudes of the team members impacted by the change. Better alignment between the change and the change leadership approach directly impacts team members' commitment levels.

4. **Reduce Complexity & Prototype Change:** Conduct a change pilot or "prototype" of the new way of doing things to demonstrate what success will look like. Once team members have a clear picture of what to expect, it will be easier for them to mirror and model the behaviors required to achieve those outcomes.

5. **Increase Try-ability:** Present examples of what expected behaviors and actions are needed to support the change using training, scenarios, use cases, and role-playing to boost team members' familiarity with new ways of doing things.

Consistency: What behaviors and actions do we need to role model to ensure our words match our intent? Those leading the change demonstrate role modelling and trust-building behaviors that increase support for the change.

1. **Coaching Leaders:** Coach leaders in ways they can be seen as change role models and champions (e.g., recognizing and rewarding behaviors).

2. **Be patient:** In an age of Agile Change Management rapid transformation, there are more temptations than ever to rush change. Do not give into that temptation. Sell change effectively by giving team members to reasonable time and space to change. Understand that different people will adapt to change at different rates.

3. **Foster Trust:** Leaders who are seen as consistent, reliable, and dedicated to the change effort have an advantage over those who are not. Create 'small win' opportunities where leaders can demonstrate their ability to align their words to their actions in order to build/maintain change momentum.

4. **Participation:** The research showed that information and participation change leadership had equally beneficial effects on change commitment. Participation can be fostered in several ways, including creating opportunities for team members to envision possibilities for the future, solve important change-related challenges, and develop solutions.

5. **Observability:** Not long after the change process is initiated, successful change leaders understand the importance of clearly demonstrating the results of the change and "early wins". Without this, team members can begin to lose heart if they see few benefits resulting from the change.

6. **Create (positive) History:** Closely related to "observability", organizations with a history of poor change results need to invest more time and energy into changing the change narrative and creating wins. Openly address past failures (do not hide them) and articulate the reasons behind why those failures occurred. Once defined, reset expectations by explaining what will be different and create new metrics for measuring success and failure.

As you use the above 2IsC™ elements to craft the ideal change messages for your team and organization, you may also find it helpful to conduct an audit of your organization's readiness for transformational change. An example of how one company adopted the 2IsC™ model to create a more customer-centric culture across multiple project phases is presented in Figure 13.

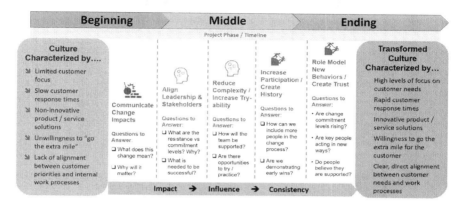

Figure 13. Customer-focused culture change: beginning, middle, end

Bringing it all together

At the core of 2IsC™ change is the focus on outcomes. While there are a number of factors to consider when thinking about how to communicate and effectively lead change in your organization, the fact is having a clear message about where your organization needs to move and finding ways to consistently support that message are among the top ways change leaders effectively lead their organizations. By selecting the right change factors for their organization, change leaders can generate the levels of commitment needed to transition through each stage of the change journey.

Concluding Thoughts

"The only way to get ahead is to find errors in conventional wisdom."

Larry Ellison

Throughout the pages of this book I have tried to make the case that the key differentiator between organizations and teams that change successfully is the critical mass of people who are committed to making changes. I've used the term highly engaged commitment to refer to what is known in the academic research as affective commitment to change. These are people who make changes to their workplace behaviors and practices not simply because they feel they have to or because they have been told to, but because they actually want to make these changes and believe in the goals and outcomes of the change initiatives of which they are apart. In short, these are the people who change because they actually want to. These are the committed "true believers" so to speak. Research on this topic shows the gap between leader-proposed organizational transformations and team members who believe in the underlying goals and objectives of those transformations is often quite small. Why then are so many organizational transformations unsuccessful? I contend the reason for this is, too often, change leaders initiate, communicate, and lead organizational changes in ways that do not comport with the way their teams need to hear those messages to trigger and sustain highly engaged change commitment. In other words, they do not effectively sell commitment to change. The result is what I call zombie organizational changes in which everyone goes through the motions of change and transformation without producing meaningful emotional, behavioral, or mental shifts. The result is change resistance in all its forms, be it subtle or more overt. This leads to a negative downward spiral since research shows that resistance in previous change initiatives results in higher levels of resistance in subsequent change efforts. To counter this effect and to initiate and sustain large scale organizational changes in ways that result in commitment rather than resistance, change leaders need to focus on five researched-based factors that have been shown to predict highly engaged change commitment. These are:

- Impact
- Information-based Change Leadership
- Participation-based Change Leadership
- Trust in Management
- Change Capability and Capacity

Each of these are summarized in the 2IsC™ Model. Leaders who incorporate these factors into their change leadership approaches increase highly engaged commitment levels and increase the likelihood of change success. This is especially true for change initiatives that involve people. As we explored in chapter 1, the top two highest change/transformation risk factors are people and commitment related. Change initiatives with higher rates of people involvement carry significantly higher risks and, in my experience, there are few, if any, large scale transformation efforts that do not involve people. To adequately plan for and lead change, leaders need to

The future of effective organizational change leadership will be individuals who can lead with clear and transparent information while engaging workers throughout each stage of the change journey.

understand that change costs come in two forms--one financial (e.g., the financial costs of change) and people costs (e.g., the time and effort associated with commitment). This book focused on the second half of that equation and the need for change leaders reduce change costs by selling change in ways that reduce people costs. The future of effective organizational change leadership will be individuals who can lead with clear and transparent information while engaging workers throughout each stage of the change journey.

Team members who are given the necessary information about the "what" of change and have opportunities to create the "how", will be more engaged in the change process and more willing to commit to and buy into workplace change.

Thinking Differently About Change

Change leadership skills are needed more than ever in today's operating environment. Often it's a 'change or die situation' and leaders who understand how to leverage Impact, Influence, and Consistency will set themselves and their organizations apart. Change models that do not account for impact, influence and commitment will become less relevant in the context of rapid change with ambiguous goals. Increasing customer satisfaction, improving revenue, and becoming more innovative are all examples of ambiguous change goals that require interrelated sets of complex tasks and judgement. Should we use approach A or B or with this client versus a different client? Should we provide a customized solution or a standard approach? The path toward achieving these results are unclear and often require judgment, assessment of multiple outcomes, if-then scenarios, and, above all, commitment from a critical mass of stakeholders across a range of departments, functions, and organizational silos.

In a world where it is increasingly difficult to command or demand compliance, effective change leaders understand that their number one job is to sell change in a way that most effectively conveys how the new approach to doing things will meet customer, internal team member, and purposeful, social goals. Effective change leaders align increasingly complex operations to make it easy for their teams to navigate needed organizational changes, improve the value of internal and external interactions, and reduce low-impact, unnecessary administrative activities.

Whether your organization is undergoing a survival focused transformation or a growth and innovation-focused transformation to ensure continued success, the same principles of selling change--using impact, influence, and consistency--will apply. The reality is that it is all but impossible to "manage" any but the most simplistic organizational changes. It is however very possible to lead organizational changes in ways that put the odds of change success in your favor. Too many well-planned and superbly executed change initiatives fail to deliver their expected results because they fail to consider the vital role commitment plays in the change journey. Too many change leaders are using antiquated approaches to leading change within and across their organizations and too many workers are feeling tired and burnt out from going through the motions of change without real commitment. While most people have a hunch that commitment is important, few leaders understand its importance in the change management process or how to increase it. I wrote this book to fill that gap. Organizational changes that are rooted in commitment have higher rates of success and engagement. My research (and the results of over 650 survey participants) reveals that it is possible to get people to commit to organizational changes even when the personal risks and threats of those changes are high. The key to selling change is to approach it in the ways that work. Throughout this book we have examined case studies, research, and organizational examples that demonstrate communicating the need for organizational change using impact, influence, and consistency creates buy-in across organizational levels and results in highly engaged commitment. This commitment translates into meaningful alignment towards and engagement with organizational changes.

One way to think about the challenge of organizational change and transformation is mastering two different change leadership types. To succeed in any transformation, your organization must be able to develop new ideas, processes, ventures and ways of thinking. Additionally, you must be able spread these ideas and processes through the organization.

As a change leader, you must become skilled at 'impact-focused communications' (nurturing new ideas and change directions) and 'outcome-focused communications' (integrating new mindsets and ways of working into your organization's culture and operations). Without an impact focus, change initiatives lack the spark needed to get the leadership team, middle managers, and team members aligned to and supportive of the change. Without an outcome focus, change initiatives fail to take root and generate meaningful difference for your organization.

Change leaders who will flourish in the future will be those who are able to combine the right strategic mindset with the right change leadership skills. They will understand the new strategic fundamentals of their organization and use those to craft new products, services, brands and business models (see chapter 6). Whatever the organization size, they will maintain the organizational agility to seize new opportunities and do so by balancing classic change management-focused communications with the ability to cascade transformation throughout the entire organization, maintaining momentum along the way. Supporting change leaders in this effort will be a cadre of research, tools, change data, and models that will enable them to focus on the right mix of impact, influence, and consistency focused factors at the right times throughout the change and transformation cycle.

Today, amid constant organizational change, no organization can thrive for long just adhering to antiquated assumptions about what enables effective change and transformation. The need for change necessitates the need to determine what will work to gain commitment and buy-in to those changes. Effective change management can be thought of as the continuous cycle of the behaviors, communications, and actions needed to support an outcomes-focused change strategy. This will require new ways of thinking about leading change. The revolution in change leadership is still just getting started. With an ever-unfolding cascade of new technologies and organizational disruptors and all the threats (and potential) they represent, it is practically impossible to predict exactly how the future will impact your organization or any industry. But if you are savvy, you can adapt your change leadership approach to align to each new wave of change as an opportunity to create new value on your team and transform your organization.

Excelsior!

Acknowledgements

Although one name appears on the cover, the people, ideas, and influences that combine to produce a book like this are many. I am grateful to my wife and two sons for their support and forbearance while I wrote this book. Previous co-workers and the Lieutenant Commander who took the time to engage with me in lengthy discussions about leadership, management, hard data, "squishy outcomes" and 'black swan' events. The students I had the opportunity to teach at Accenture's Core Analyst School, the graduate students at the University of Minnesota who took my class and faculty who helped me understand what I was really doing and bring the requisite rigor to my research and analysis. "Scotty" and the risk-taking HR and talent leaders like him who allowed a doctoral student to ask their employees some tough questions and were willing to champion my work in their organizations. Special thanks to Professor Ken Bartlett, my advisor, who helped 'bring me over the finish line' through a combination of tough facts and practical tips. My comrade on the journey, and fellow coffee snob, Jane. The ones who pushed me to soar like an eagle by teaching me "the art of the possible". Thanks also to Dr. Timothy McClernon for his detailed review and feedback on an early draft of the book manuscript and the intellectual giants on whose shoulders I stand including Dr. David Szabla and Professors Theresa Glomb, Tahira Probst, John Meyer, David Herold, Donald Fedor, and Andrew Van de Ven, for influencing my thinking on these important topics, and finally, the Managing Directors (Partners), consulting colleagues and numerous Private Sector and Federal clients around the world during my time at Accenture who, by allowing me to help them solve their most pressing people problems, unwittingly prodded me into creating research-based tools to improve the ways organizations change.

Notes

Introduction

[1] R. "Ray" Wang, "Disrupting Digital Business: Create an Authentic Experience in the Peer-to-Peer Economy." *Harvard Business Review Press*, May 2015.

[2] Mauldin, John. Don't Be So Sure That States Can't Go Bankrupt. *Forbes*. Retrieved 28 July 2017 from https://www.forbes.com/sites/johnmauldin/2016/07/28/dont-be-so-sure-that-states-cant-go-bankrupt/#1af7949a2f2d

[3] Ron Ashkenas, "Change management needs to change," Harvard Business Review, April 16, 2013, https://hbr.org/2013/04/change-management-needs-to-cha.

[4] Scott Anthony, Clark G. Gilbert, and Mark W. Johnson (2017). *Dual Transformation: How to Reposition Today's Business While Creating the Future*. Harvard Business Review Press.

[5] John P. Kotter (2014). *Accelerate: Building Strategic Agility for a Faster-Moving World*. Harvard Business Review Press.

[6] 2010 Intuit 2020 Report: Twenty Trends that will Shape the Next Decade. Intuit. Retrieved from http://http-download.intuit.com/http.intuit/CMO/intuit/futureofsmallbusiness/intuit_2020_report.pdf

[7] iSpot.tv (2017). Uber TV Commercial, 'Side Hustle: Earning' Song by Saint Motel. *iSpot.tv* https://www.ispot.tv/ad/wOYe/uber-side-hustle-earning-song-by-saint-motel

[8] Brown, Anna (2016). Key findings about the American workforce and the changing job market. *Pew Research Center*. Retrieved May 5, 2017 from http://www.pewresearch.org/fact-tank/2016/10/06/key-findings-about-the-american-workforce-and-the-changing-job-market/

[9] The Undercover Recruiter. A Guide to the Future of Work, with Josh Bersin. Retrieved from https://theundercoverrecruiter.com/guide-future-work/

[10] Meister, Jeanne. The Employee Experience Is The Future Of Work: 10 HR Trends For 2017. Forbes 06 January 2017. Retrieved from https://www.forbes.com/sites/jeannemeister/2017/01/05/the-employee-experience-is-the-future-of-work-10-hr-trends-for-2017/#72a2dade20a6

[11] Shin, Laura. Work From Home In 2017: The Top 100 Companies Offering Remote Jobs. Forbes. Retrieved https://www.forbes.com/sites/laurashin/2017/01/31/work-from-home-in-2017-the-top-100-companies-offering-remote-jobs/#35d0d49642d8

[12] Loudenback, Tanza. More tech companies have stopped keeping employee salaries secret — and they're seeing results. *Business Insider*. Retrieved from http://www.businessinsider.com/why-companies-have-open-salaries-and-pay-transparency-2017-4

[13] Harvard Business Review. Home Unimprovement: Was Nardelli's Tenure at Home Depot a Blueprint for Failure? http://knowledge.wharton.upenn.edu/article/home-unimprovement-was-nardellis-tenure-at-home-depot-a-blueprint-for-failure/

[14] CNN Money. Nasser Out as Ford CEO. http://money.cnn.com/2001/10/30/ceos/ford/

[15] Prashant Bordia, Elizabeth Jones, Cindy Gallois, Victor J. Callan and Nicholas DiFonzo (2006). Management are Aliens!: Rumors and Stress During Organizational Change. *Group Organization Management*, 31, 601-620.

[16] Chapter 1 - Change in the Real World Maurer, R. (2010). Why 70% of Change Fail. Retrieved from http://www.reply-mc.com/2010/09/19/why-70-of-changes-fail-by-rick-maurer/

[17] IBM (2008). Making Change Work.

[18] CIO (2017). Why IT projects still fail. Retrieved from: https://www.cio.com/article/3211485/project-management/why-it-projects-still-fail.html?upd=1508776560384

[19] Practical Change Management (2011). Right Investment, Right Impact: Creating a Change Management Budget Retrieved from: http://practicalchangemanagement.blogspot.com/2011/05/right-investment-right-impact-creating.html

[20] Gartner, March 2011. Lessons from 169 SAP Implementations Using Service Providers in North America.

[21] Venkatesh, V., & Davis, F. D. (2000). A theoretical extension of the technology acceptance model: Four longitudinal field studies. Management Science, 46(2), 186-204. doi:10.1287/mnsc.46.2.186.11926

[22] Venkatesh, Viswanath; Morris, Michael G.; Davis, Gordon B.; Davis, Fred D. (2003-01-01). "User Acceptance of Information Technology: Toward a Unified View". MIS Quarterly. 27 (3): 425–478. JSTOR 30036540.

[23] KPMG (2015). Evidence-based HR: The bridge between your people and delivering business Strategy. Retrieved from https://assets.kpmg.com/content/dam/kpmg/pdf/2015/04/evidence-based-hr.pdf

[24] Boushey, Heather and Glynn, Sarah (2012). There Are Significant Business Costs to Replacing Employees. Retrieved from https://www.americanprogress.org/issues/economy/reports/2012/11/16/44464/there-are-significant-business-costs-to-replacing-employees/

[25] Chapter 2 Faulty Change Assumptions Kotter, John. Leading Change. Boston: Harvard Business Review Press. https://www.amazon.com/dp/B00A07FPEO/ref=dp-kindle-redirect?_encoding=UTF8&btkr=1

[26] Prosci (2017). *Applications of ADKAR*. Retrieved July 26, 2017 from https://www.prosci.com/adkar/applications-of-adkar

[27] Rock, D. (2008, March). SCARF: a brain-based model for collaborating with and influencing others. *NeuroLeadership Journal*. Retrieved July 20, 2017, from https://www.epa.gov/sites/production/files/2015-09/documents/thurs_georgia_9_10_915_covello.pdf

[28] McLeod, S. (2016). *Maslow's hierarchy of needs*. Retrieved July 20, 2017 https://www.simplypsychology.org/maslow.html

[29] Clampitt, P., DeKoch, R., & Cashman, T. (2000). A strategy for communicating about uncertainty. *Academy of Management Executive*, Vol. 14, No. 4.

[30] Deloitte (2017). *The Deloitte Millennial Survey 2017.* Retrieved July 24, 2017 from https://www2.deloitte.com/global/en/pages/about-deloitte/articles/millennialsurvey.html

[31] McKinsey & Co. (April 2009). The irrational side of change management. The McKinsey Quarterly. Retrieved May 15, 2017 from http://www.mckinsey.com/business-functions/organization/our-insights/the-irrational-side-of-change-management

[32] Chapter 3 - A Research Story (The Making of a Change Commitment Model) Parish, J. T., Cadwallader, S., and Bush, P. (2007). Want to, need to, ought to: employee commitment to organizational change. Journal of Organizational Change Management, 21(1), 32-52.

[33] Smith, Robert E. (2013). Insecure commitment and resistance: an examination of change leadership, self-efficacy, and trust on the relationship between job insecurity, employee commitment, and resistance to organizational change. Retrieved from the University of Minnesota Digital Conservancy, http://hdl.handle.net/11299/161089.

[34] Miller, V. D., Johnson, J. R., and Grau, J. (1994). Antecedents to willingness to participate in a planned organizational change. *Journal of Applied Communication Research*, 22(1994), 59-80.

[35] Szabla, D. B. (2007). A Multidimensional View of Resistance to Organizational Change: Exploring Cognitive, Emotional, and Intentional Responses to Planned Change Across Perceived Change Leadership Strategies. *Human Resource Development Quarterly*, 18(4), 525-558.

[36] Correlations between

[37] Fedor, D. B., & Herold, D. M. (2004). Effects of Change and Change Management on Employee Responses: An Overview of Results from Multiple Studies. *Tappi Fall 2004 Technical Conference*, 3-1

[38] Isen, A. M., & Daubman, K. A. (1984). The influence of affect on categorization. *Journal of Personality and Social Psychology*, 47(6), 1206-1217. http://dx.doi.org/10.1037/0022-3514.47.6.1206

[39] R. E. Petty, D. W. Schumann, S. A. Richman, and A.J. Strathman, "Positive Mood and Persuasion: Different Roles for Affect Under High- and Low Elaboration Conditions," Journal of Personality and Social Psychology 64 (1993): 5–20

[40] Cole, M. S., Bruch, H. and Vogel, B. (2006), Emotion as mediators of the relations between perceived supervisor support and psychological hardiness on employee cynicism. *Journal of Organizational Behavior*, 27(4), 463–484. doi:10.1002/job.381

[41] Evangelia Demerouti, Despoina Xanthopoulou & Arnold B. Bakker (2017). How do cynical employees serve their customers? A multi-method study. European Journal of Work and Organizational Psychology, Pages 1-12

[42] Danzinger, S., Levav, J., & Avnaim-Pesso, L. (2011). Extraneous factors in judicial decisions.

[43] Driskell, J. E., Copper, C., & Moran, A. (1994). Does mental practice enhance performance? *Journal of Applied Psychology*, 79(4), 481-492. http://dx.doi.org/10.1037/0021-9010.79.4.481

[44] Wanberg, C. R., & Banas, J. T. (2000). Predictors and outcomes of openness to changes in a reorganizing workplace. Journal of Applied Psychology, 85(1), 132-142.

[45] Beer, M. (1980). Organizational change and development: A systems view. Santa Monica, CA: Goodyear.

[46] Black, J.S.; Gregersen, H.B. (1997). "Participative Decision-Making: An Integration of Multiple Dimensions". Human Relations. 50: 859–878. doi:10.1177/001872679705000705.

[47] Insert change curve reference here

[48] Zak, Paul. *Harvard Business Review* (January-February 2017). The Neuroscience of Trust: Management Behaviors that Foster Employee Engagement.

[49] Elliot, A., (2008). Handbook of Approach and Avoidance Motivation. Psychology Press

[50] Burns, J. M. (1978). Leadership. New York: Harper & Row.

[51] Sashkin, M. (2004). Transformational leadership approaches: A review and synthesis. In J. Antonakis, A. T. Cianciolo, & R. J. Sternberg (Eds.), The nature of leadership (pp. 171–196). Thousand Oaks, CA: Sage.

[52] Bass, B. M. (1985). Leadership and performance beyond expectations. New York: Free Press.

[53] Herold, David & B Fedor, Donald & Caldwell, Steven & Liu, Yi. (2008). The Effects of Transformational and Change Leadership on Employees'

Commitment to a Change: A Multilevel Study. The Journal of applied psychology. 93. 346-57. 10.1037/0021-9010.93.2.346.

[54] Stéphanie Mingardon, Meldon Wolfgang, Perry Keenan, Audélia Krief, Annabel Doust, and Florence Adida. August 9, 2017. Digital-Era Change Runs on People Power. Retrieved from https://www.bcg.com/en-us/publications/2017/change-management-organization-digital-era-change-runs-people-power.aspx

[55] Sverke, M., Hellgren, J., & Näswall, K. (2002). No security: A meta-analysis and review of job insecurity and its consequences. *Journal of Occupational Health Psychology, 7*(3), 242–264.

[56] Reisel, W. D., Probst, T. M., Chia, S., Malolores, III, C. M., & Kong, C. J. (2010). The effects of job insecurity on job satisfaction, organizational citizenship behavior, deviant behavior, and negative emotions of employees. *International Studies of Management & Organization, 40*(1), 74-91.

[57] Chapter 4 - Using Impact and Influence to Sell Change Hochman, G., & Yechiam, E. (2011). Loss aversion in the eye and in the heart: The Autonomic Nervous System's responses to losses. Journal of Behavioral Decision Making, 24, 140-156.

[58] Simply Psychology (2014). Cognitive Dissonance. Retrieved from https://www.simplypsychology.org/cognitive-dissonance.html

[59] Harvard Business Review (2012). Cultural Change That Sticks. http://knowledge.wharton.upenn.edu/article/home-unimprovement-was-nardellis-tenure-at-home-depot-a-blueprint-for-failure/

[60] Zak, Paul. *Harvard Business Review* (January-February 2017). The Neuroscience of Trust: Management Behaviors that Foster Employee Engagement.

[61] Pornpitakpan, C. (2006). The Persuasiveness of Source Credibility: A Critical Review of Five Decades' Evidence. Journal of Applied Psychology, 34(2).

[62] Simply Psychology (2007). The Milgram Experiment. Retrieved from https://www.simplypsychology.org/milgram.html

[63] Peter Aldhous (2009). *New Scientist*. Humans prefer cockiness to expertise. https://www.newscientist.com/article/mg20227115.500-humans-prefer-cockiness-to-expertise/

[64] Families and Work Institute (2008). Retail Industry Employees and Turnover. Retrieved from http://familiesandwork.org/downloads/TurnoverAndRetail.pdf

[65] Psychological Bulletin (2015). Appealing to Fear: A Meta-Analysis of Fear Appeal Effectiveness and Theories. Retrieved from https://www.apa.org/pubs/journals/releases/bul-a0039729.pdf

[66] Niccolò Machiavelli (1469-1527) was an Italian Renaissance era historian, politician, diplomat, philosopher, humanist, and writer often called the founder of modern political science

[67] NPR (2013). Why We Care More About Losses Than Gains. Retrieved from:

[68] Jeffrey D. Berejikian & Bryan R. Early (2013). Loss Aversion and Foreign Policy Resolve. http://onlinelibrary.wiley.com/doi/10.1111/pops.12012/abstract

[69] Kiefer, T. (2005). Feeling bad: antecedents and consequences of negative emotions in ongoing change. *Journal of Organizational Behavior*, 26(8), 875-897.

[70] Friedman, Ron. *The Best Place to Work: The Art and Science of Creating an Extraordinary Workplace*. USA: TarcherPerigee, 2014.

[71] Lynn, M. (1991). Scarcity effects on value: A quantitative review of the commodity theory literature. Psychology & Marketing, 8(1), 43-57.

[72] Chapter 5 - 2IsC™(Impact, Influence, & Consistency) in Action Wikipedia Retrieved 29 July 2017 from https://en.wikipedia.org/wiki/NYU_Langone_Medical_Center

[73] McNulty, Eric, Foote, Nathaniel, Wilson, Douglas. "Management Lessons from One Hospital's Dramatic Turnaround." *Strategy + Business.* 13 March 2017. Retrieved 14 May 2017 from https://www.strategy-business.com/article/Management-Lessons-from-One-Hospitals-Dramatic-Turnaround

[74] Ghosn, Carlos. "Saving the Business Without Losing the Company." Harvard Business Review. January 2002. Retrieved 14 July 2017 from https://hbr.org/2002/01/saving-the-business-without-losing-the-company

[75] Ghosn, Carlos. "Saving the Business Without Losing the Company." Harvard Business Review. January 2002. Retrieved 14 July 2017 from https://hbr.org/2002/01/saving-the-business-without-losing-the-company

[76] Woodyard, Chris. "Carlos Ghosn Stepping Down as CEO of Nissan." USAToday, 22 Feb, 2017. Retrieved 14 July 2017 from https://www.usatoday.com/story/money/cars/2017/02/22/carlos-ghosn-stepping-down-nissan-ceo/98278024/

[77] Lauby, Sharlyn. "Organizations Can Make Their Brand MORE Than it is Today." *Great Place to Work Blog.* 22 March 2017, https://www.greatplacetowork.com/blog/628-organizations-can-make-their-brand-more-than-it-is-today?highlight=WyJidWlsZC1hLWJlYXIiLCJidWlsZC1hLWJlYXIincyJd

[78] Weiderman, Greta. "Build-A-Bear reports $49 million loss in 2012." St Louis Business Jourpnal. 22 March 2017, http://www.bizjournals.com/stlouis/morning_call/2013/02/build-a-bear-reports-49-million-loss.html

[79] Carol, Haley. "Build-A-Bear CEO Shares Her Secret to Turnaround Success." Great Place to Work Blog. 09 May 2016. Retrieved 16 May

2017 from https://www.greatplacetowork.com/blog/147-build-a-bear-ceo-shares-her-secret-to-turnaround-success?highlight=WyJidWlsZCIs ImEiLCInYSIsImJlYXIiLCJidWlsZCBhIiwiYnVpbGQgYSBiZWFyIiwiYSBi ZWFyIl0=

[80] Fedor, D. B., & Herold, D. M. (2004). Effects of Change and Change Management on Employee Responses: An Overview of Results from Multiple Studies. *Tappi Fall 2004 Technical Conference*, 3-1

[81] Hochman, G., & Yechiam, E. (2011). Loss aversion in the eye and in the heart: The Autonomic Nervous System's responses to losses. *Journal of Behavioral Decision Making*, 24, 140-156.

[82] John, Sharon P. (2015). "Meet the woman who rescued Build-A-Bear Workshop". Fortune. 23 March 2017, http://fortune.com/2015/07/14/ sharon-price-john-dealing-with-change/

[83] Can Build-A-Bear Workshop Bounce Back After Last Week's 16% Drop? Retrieved from https://www.fool.com/investing/2017/02/20/can-build-a-bear-workshop-bounce-back-after-last-w.aspx

[84] Business Insider, 2014. How Chipotle Founder Steve Ells Got The Idea To Sell Burritos. Retrieved from http://www.businessinsider.com/ chipotle-founder-steve-ells-idea-2014-3

[85] The Motley Fool (2016). Why a Chipotle Mexican Grill Turnaround is All But Inevitable. Retrieved from https://www.fool.com/ investing/2016/10/16/why-a-chipotle-mexican-grill-turnaround-is-all-but.aspx

[86] David Goldman (July 26, 2017). Chipotle says sick employee responsible for latest outbreak. CNN Money. Retrieved from http://money.cnn. com/2017/07/26/news/companies/chipotle-sick/index.html

[87] Zacks Equity Research (December 21, 2017). Chipotle (CMG) Faces Fresh Investigation, Shares Decline. Retrieved from https://www.zacks.

com/stock/news/286689/chipotle-cmg-faces-fresh-investigation-shares-decline?cid=CS-CNN-HL-286689

[88] Harvard Business Review (2017). Box's CEO on Pivoting to the Enterprise Market. https://hbr.org/ideacast/2017/12/boxs-ceo-on-pivoting-to-the-enterprise-market

[89] Anna Mazarakis and Alyson Shontell, July 14, 2017. 'I was having nightmares for a few weeks': Box CEO Aaron Levie reveals how hard it was to build a $2.5 billion business and take it public by age 29. Business Insider.

Made in the USA
Monee, IL
21 February 2020

22142035R00095